Family Circle

Pancakes
Pikelets, Crepes and Waffles

The Family Circle® Promise of Success

Welcome to the world of Confident Cooking,
created for you in the Australian **Family Circle®
Test Kitchen,** where recipes are double-tested by
our team of home economists to achieve a
high standard of success—and delicious
results every time.

MURDOCH BOOKS®
Sydney • London • Vancouver • New York

C O N T E

Lemon and Banana Pancakes, page 11

Chicken Pancakes with Char-grilled Vegetables and Feta,
page 22

Cheddar Blinis with Roasted Cherry Tomatoes and Pesto,
page 44

Hash Brown Waffles, page 103

The test kitchen where our recipes are double-tested by our team of home economists to achieve a high standard of success and delicious results every time.

Crispy Vermicelli Pikelets with Sesame Vegetables, page 50

The Publisher thanks the following for their assistance in the photography for this book: Wardlaw Fabrics; Windsor Antique Market; Birkenhead Antique Market; Cambur; Gempo; Villeroy & Boch; Waterford Wedgwood; Royal Doulton; Corso de' Fiori; Pacific East India Company; Home and Garden on the Mall; Storehouse; Parterre Garden; Redelman Fabrics; Made in Japan; Le Forge.

Gravlax Pikelets with Red Capsicum and Tomato Coulis, page 48

When we test our recipes, we rate them for ease of preparation. The following cookery ratings are on the recipes in this book, making them easy to use and understand.

A single Cooking with Confidence symbol indicates a recipe that is simple and generally quick to make —perfect for beginners.

Two symbols indicate the need for just a little more care and a little more time.

Three symbols indicate special dishes that need more investment in time, care and patience—but the results are worth it.

Front cover: Blueberry Pancakes, page 10; Capsicum Pikelets with Prosciutto, page 55; Hazelnut Praline Crepes with Chocolate Sauce, page 63

Inside front cover: Boozy Fruit Pikelets and Blueberry Pikelets, page 36

Ricotta Pikelets with Roasted Walnuts and Maple Syrup, page 32

Orange and Passionfruit Waffles with Lemon Curd, page 94

The Perfect Treat

Pancakes, pikelets, crepes and waffles are a delicious choice for any mealtime, whether it's breakfast, lunch or supper. This short guide to preparation and cooking will enable you to make a satisfying meal or a sweet special treat with outstanding results.

MAKING BATTERS

Pancakes, pikelets, crepes and waffles are all made from batters containing varying quantities of flour, eggs and milk. There is a basic recipe for each at the beginning of the chapters. A good batter is essential, and by following these simple procedures, you will get a great result every time.

Sift the dry ingredients (flours, spices, sugar or raising agents) into a bowl and mix together. Make a well in the centre with a wooden spoon, and add the combined eggs and milk or other liquids (often melted butter, fruit juice or essence) and flavourings (rinds, chocolate and nuts), either gradually or all at once, depending on the instructions in the recipe.

Use a whisk or wooden spoon to combine the liquid with the dry

Make a well in the centre of the dry ingredients with a wooden spoon.

Pour the liquid mixture into the well and slowly combine with the dry ingredients.

Crepes should be paper thin and have delicate lacy edges.

ingredients, drawing them in slowly from the edge of the well. It is important not to overmix the batter as this will cause the pancake to be tough and leathery. The batter can also be made in a food processor. Process in short bursts in order to avoid overmixing.

Traditionally, pikelet batter is made by stirring all the ingredients together until just moistened. This leaves lumps in the batter, which is the correct texture to achieve a light fluffy pikelet. Some recipes in this book, however, ask for the batter to be stirred or whisked until just smooth. This does not mean that the pikelet will be tough, just that a different result is required for that recipe.

For crepe batters, whisk the liquid gradually into the dry ingredients until smooth. The batter can then be left to rest for up to 2 hours. Resting the batter enables the flour particles to expand in the liquid, and produces a lighter, more tender crepe. The crepe batter should always be of a pouring consistency. A traditional crepe has delicate lacy edges and should be thin enough to read a love letter through.

Waffle batter should be thick enough to spread evenly over the heated waffle iron without it running over the edges. The batter can be made plain or with added flavourings.

PANS

The most expensive and impressive looking pans are not necessarily the best. If you only make crepes occasionally, and do not wish to splash out on an expensive crepe pan, a small frying pan is a good cost-effective alternative. Electric crepe makers also work very well.

Pancakes and pikelets can be cooked in a crepe pan, although a larger frying pan will allow you to cook more pikelets in each batch. Choose the size and type of frying pan

A small non-stick frying pan is a good substitute for an expensive crepe pan.

that is most suitable to your needs, from the cast iron, stainless steel and non-stick varieties that are available.

Waffle irons come in varying sizes and designs. Some of the older jaffle irons have removable plates. These

You can also make successful crepes using an electric crepe maker.

come with both waffle and jaffle plates. Most of the waffle makers available in department stores nowadays are electric.

SEASONING THE PAN

This technique is used to prepare the pan for cooking crepes, and is usually only required for cast iron and some stainless steel pans. Warm a small amount of salt in the pan and rub into

Season the pan by warming some salt and rubbing it into the base.

Remove the salt and grease the base with some butter wrapped in a paper towel.

the base with paper towels. The salt will begin to discolour. Discard the salt and repeat the process three times, then wipe the pan clean. Next, lightly grease the pan, using a little butter wrapped in a paper towel to avoid overgreasing, and the pan is ready to use. This process creates a smooth surface on which to cook the crepes and prevents them sticking.

COOKING

Pancakes vary in thickness. Some can be almost as thin as a crepe, others as fat as a pikelet—similar to an American flapjack or hotcake. Pancakes and pikelets are usually made the same way. Spoon or pour

the required amount of batter into a lightly greased, heated pan. When bubbles begin to appear and just break on the surface, use a spatula to

As bubbles start to break on the surface, turn the pikelet over with a spatula.

turn them over (the underside should be golden) and cook the other side. Pancakes and pikelets will need to be cooked in several batches depending on the size of pan you are using.

A crepe batter should always pour easily, and a little more milk should be added to the batter if it does not. Heat and lightly grease the required pan. Pour a little batter into the heated pan, swirling to ensure the base of the pan is thinly coated with batter. Quickly pour any excess back into the jug before placing over the heat. Cook for about 1 minute, or until the edges start to curl slightly. Use a palette knife or spatula to loosen the edges, then flip the crepe and cook the other side for about 1 minute. The first couple of crepes sometimes stick, so thin the batter with a little milk or water if you find it is too thick.

When the crepe is cooked, the edges will curl slightly.

As soon as pancakes, pikelets and crepes are cooked on both sides, transfer them to a plate and cover with a tea towel to keep them moist.

If the waffle batter is thick, spread it over the plate with the back of a spoon.

To cook waffles, preheat the waffle maker and brush the heated grid with a little melted butter or oil. Pour the required amount of batter into the centre of the waffle grid. If the batter is thick, quickly spread it with the back of a spoon right up to the edge of the plate. Close the lid and cook for the specified time, or until the waffles are golden and slightly crisp. The amount of batter you will need to use for each waffle may vary slightly according to the size of waffle maker that you have. The proportions will differ between brands.

STORAGE

Pancakes, pikelets, crepes and waffles all tend to be best eaten on the day they are made. But if necessary, they can be stored in the following ways.

Pancakes and pikelets can be made, cooled and stored, sealed in an airtight container, in the refrigerator or in a cool dry place for up to 2 days. They can be reheated successfully in the microwave oven on High (100%) for 30 seconds to 1 minute, before serving.

Crepes can also be made in advance and stored, layered alternately with sheets of greaseproof paper or plastic wrap. Store either in an airtight container or in plastic bags in the refrigerator for 1 week, or the freezer for 4 weeks. Thaw before using.

Cooked waffles can be cooled and stored in airtight plastic bags in the freezer for up to 4 weeks. Allow them to thaw just slightly before you re-crisp them under a preheated grill, in a toaster or in a moderate oven for 10–15 minutes before serving. If using an oven, you may wish to cover the waffles loosely with foil to prevent them drying out.

PANCAKES

PANCAKE STACK WITH WHIPPED BUTTER AND MAPLE SYRUP

Preparation time: 5 minutes
  + 20 minutes standing
Total cooking time: 15–20 minutes
Makes 9 pancakes

1¹/2 cups (185 g/6 oz)
   self-raising flour
1 teaspoon baking powder
2 tablespoons caster sugar
pinch of salt
2 eggs, lightly beaten
1 cup (250 ml/8 fl oz) milk
60 g (2 oz) butter, melted
100 g (3¹/3 oz) butter,
   whipped (with electric
   beaters or a wooden spoon)
maple syrup, to serve

1 Sift the flour, baking powder, sugar and salt into a bowl and make a well in the centre. Mix together the eggs, milk and butter in a jug and pour into the well all at once, whisking to form a smooth batter. Cover the bowl with plastic wrap and set the batter aside for 20 minutes.

2 Heat a frying pan and brush lightly with melted butter or oil. Pour ¹/4 cup (60 ml/2 fl oz) batter into the pan and swirl gently to create a pancake about 10 cm (4 inches) in diameter. Cook over low heat for 1 minute, or until the underside is golden.

3 Turn the pancake over and cook the other side very quickly, for about 10 seconds. Transfer to a plate and keep warm while cooking the remaining batter. Serve the pancakes stacked, warm or cold, with whipped butter and maple syrup.

Use electric beaters to whip the butter until light and creamy.

Add the egg mixture all at once to the well in the centre of the dry ingredients.

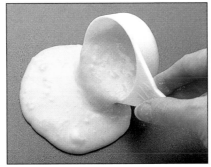

Pour ¹/4 cup (60 ml/2 fl oz) batter into the heated, greased pan.

When the underside of the pancake is golden, turn it and cook the other side.

WHOLEMEAL RAISIN PANCAKES

Preparation time: 7 minutes
+ 1–2 hours soaking
Total cooking time: 18 minutes
Makes 6 pancakes

1 cup (125 g/4 oz) raisins
1 cup (250 ml/8 fl oz) boiling
  water
3/4 cup (110 g/3²/3 oz)
  wholemeal plain flour

1 tablespoon soft brown sugar
1¹/2 teaspoons ground cinnamon
1 teaspoon baking powder
¹/2 teaspoon bicarbonate of soda
2 eggs
1 cup (250 ml/8 fl oz) milk

1 Place the raisins in a bowl, cover with the boiling water and set aside for 1–2 hours. Drain well.
2 Sift the flour into a large bowl, returning the husks to the bowl. Add the sugar, cinnamon, baking powder and bicarbonate of soda and make a well in the centre. Mix together the eggs and milk in a jug and pour into the well, stirring to form a smooth batter. Stir in the raisins.
3 Heat a frying pan (use a non-stick pan if you have one) and brush lightly with melted butter or oil. Pour ¹/2 cup (125 ml/4 fl oz) batter into the pan and cook until bubbles form and the top is slightly dry. Turn over and cook the other side until golden. Remove and keep warm while cooking the remaining batter. Serve with honey or maple syrup and fresh fruit.

Combine the sugar, cinnamon, baking powder and soda with the flour.

Soaking the raisins, before adding to the batter, will make them plumper.

Turn the pancake over when bubbles form on the surface.

Stir the sugar and choc bits into the other dry ingredients and make a well.

Use a dry bowl for beating egg whites—any grease will prevent them aerating.

Pour 1/4 cup of the batter into the heated, greased pan.

Combine all the ingredients for Hot Fudge Sauce in a pan over low heat.

CHOCOLATE CHIP PANCAKES WITH HOT FUDGE SAUCE

Preparation time: 35 minutes
Total cooking time: 30 minutes
Makes 16 pancakes

2 cups (250 g/8 oz) self-raising
 flour
2 tablespoons cocoa powder
1 teaspoon bicarbonate of soda
1/4 cup (60 g/2 oz) caster sugar
3/4 cup (130 g/41/4 oz) dark
 choc bits
1 cup (250 ml/8 fl oz) milk
1 cup (250 ml/8 fl oz) cream
2 eggs, lightly beaten
30 g (1 oz) butter, melted
3 egg whites
whipped cream or ice cream

Hot Fudge Sauce
150 g (43/4 oz) dark chocolate,
 broken into pieces
30 g (1 oz) butter
2 tablespoons light corn syrup

1/2 cup (95 g/31/4 oz) soft brown
 sugar
1/2 cup (125 ml/4 fl oz) cream

1 Sift the flour, cocoa and bicarbonate of soda into a large bowl. Stir in the sugar and choc bits and make a well in the centre. Whisk together the milk, cream, eggs and butter in a jug and gradually pour into the well and stir until just combined.

2 Beat the egg whites in a clean dry bowl until soft peaks form. Stir a heaped tablespoon of the beaten egg white into the batter to loosen it up, then lightly fold in the remaining egg white until just combined.

3 Heat a frying pan and brush lightly with melted butter or oil. Pour 1/4 cup (60 ml/2 fl oz) batter into the pan and cook over moderate heat until the underside is browned. Turn the pancake over with a spatula and cook the other side. Transfer to a plate, and cover with a tea towel while cooking the remaining batter.

4 To make Hot Fudge Sauce: Put all the ingredients in a pan and stir over low heat until melted and smooth. Serve the pancakes warm with whipped cream or ice cream and drizzled with Hot Fudge Sauce.

BLUEBERRY PANCAKES

Preparation time: 10–15 minutes
Total cooking time: 18 minutes
Makes 6 pancakes

2 cups (250 g/8 oz) plain flour
2 teaspoons baking powder
1 teaspoon bicarbonate of soda
1 teaspoon salt
1/3 cup (90 g/3 oz) sugar
2 eggs
80 g (2^2/3 oz) butter, melted
300 ml (9^2/3 fl oz) milk
2 cups (310 g/9^3/4 oz)
    blueberries, fresh or frozen

1 Sift the flour, baking powder, bicarbonate of soda and salt into a large bowl. Add the sugar and make a well in the centre. Using a fork, whisk the eggs, melted butter and milk together in a jug and pour into the well, stirring to just dampen the flour (add more milk if you prefer a thinner batter). Gently fold in the blueberries.
2 Heat a frying pan and brush lightly with melted butter or oil. Pour 1/2 cup (125 ml/4 fl oz) batter into the pan and spread out to make a pancake about 15 cm (6 inches) in diameter. Cook over low heat until bubbles appear and pop on the surface.
3 Gently turn the pancake over and cook the other side (these pancakes can be difficult to handle so take care when turning). Transfer to a plate and cover with a tea towel to keep warm while cooking the remaining batter. Delicious served warm with maple syrup, cream and fresh blueberries.

COOK'S FILE

Note: If you use frozen blueberries there is no need to defrost them.

Whisk the eggs, melted butter and milk together with a fork.

Use a metal spoon to gently fold the blueberries into the batter.

Use the back of a spoon to spread out the batter in the pan.

LEMON AND BANANA PANCAKES

Preparation time: 10–15 minutes
Total cooking time: 15 minutes
Makes 6 pancakes

1¼ cups (155 g/5 oz) self-
    raising flour, sifted
¼ cup (60 g/2 oz) sugar
½ teaspoon bicarbonate of soda
¼ teaspoon salt

finely grated rind of 1 lemon
1 cup (250 ml/8 fl oz) milk
2 eggs
2 bananas, thinly sliced
60 g (2 oz) butter, melted

1 Sift the flour, sugar, bicarbonate of soda and salt into a large bowl. Stir in the lemon rind and make a well in the centre. Whisk together the milk and eggs in a jug and pour into the well, whisking to form a smooth batter. Fold the bananas and the melted butter through the batter.

2 Heat a frying pan and brush lightly with melted butter or oil. Pour ½ cup (125 ml/4 fl oz) batter into the pan and cook the pancake until bubbles begin to appear and pop on the surface.

3 Gently turn the pancake over and cook the other side. Transfer to a plate and cover with a tea towel to keep warm while cooking the remaining batter. Delicious dusted with icing sugar and served with fresh fruit salad.

Add the lemon rind to the dry ingredients and make a well in the centre.

Fold the bananas and melted butter through the batter.

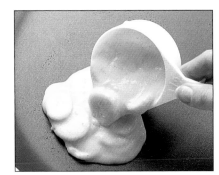
Use ½ cup of the banana batter to make each pancake.

11

SWEDISH OATMEAL PANCAKES WITH APPLE SAUCE

Preparation time: 40 minutes
+ overnight soaking
Total cooking time: 26 minutes
Makes 12 pancakes

1³/₄ cups (175 g/5²/₃ oz) rolled oats
1 cup (250 ml/8 fl oz) milk
1 cup (250 ml/8 fl oz) cream
1 kg (2 lb) apples
100 ml (3¹/₃ fl oz) water
1 tablespoon lemon juice
grated rind of ¹/₂ lemon
1 teaspoon ground cinnamon
200 g (6¹/₂ oz) sugar, plus
    2 teaspoons
100 ml (3¹/₃ fl oz) cream,
    whipped to soft peaks
¹/₂ cup (60 g/2 oz) plain flour
1¹/₂ teaspoons baking powder
2 eggs
60 g (2 oz) butter, melted

1 Mix the oats, milk and cream in a large bowl. Cover and chill overnight.
2 Peel, core and roughly chop the apples. Put the water, lemon juice, rind, cinnamon and 200 g (6¹/₂ oz) sugar in a pan, bring to the boil and stir in the apple. Cover and cook for 10 minutes. Cool slightly and purée in a food processor. Add more sugar, to taste, if necessary. Cool completely; fold in the whipped cream and chill.
3 Sift the flour and baking powder into the rolled oat mixture. Add the combined 2 teaspoons sugar, eggs and melted butter and stir until just smooth. If the mixture is too thick to pour, add a little extra milk.
4 Melt a little butter in a frying pan. Pour ¹/₄ cup (60 ml/2 fl oz) batter into the pan (you may fit 2 pancakes) and cook until the underside is golden. Turn over and cook the other side. Remove and cover with a tea towel while cooking the remaining batter. Serve warm with the apple sauce and a dusting of ground cinnamon.

COOK'S FILE

Note: The pancake batter has little sugar as the apple sauce is so sweet. If you prefer, add 3–4 tablespoons caster sugar when soaking the oats.

Bring the lemon syrup to the boil and stir in the apple pieces.

Fold the whipped cream into the cold puréed apple.

Add the combined sugar, eggs and butter to the dry ingredients.

When the underside is golden, turn the pancake over and cook the other side.

POLENTA PANCAKES WITH STRAWBERRIES AND MAPLE SYRUP

Preparation time: 15 minutes
+ 2 hours standing
Total cooking time: 30 minutes
Makes 7 pancakes

$^1/_2$ cup (75 g/2$^1/_2$ oz) finely
    ground polenta
$^1/_2$ cup (125 ml/4 fl oz) boiling
    water
$^3/_4$ cup (90 g/3 oz) plain flour
2 teaspoons baking powder
2 tablespoons caster sugar
$^1/_2$ teaspoon salt
3 eggs, lightly beaten
50 g (1$^2/_3$ oz) butter, melted
250 g (8 oz) strawberries,
    halved
maple syrup, to serve

1 Place the polenta in a large bowl, cover with the boiling water and stir until smooth. Cool slightly before adding the sifted flour, baking powder, sugar and salt. Add the eggs and mix until smooth. Stir in the melted butter. Cover and set aside for 2 hours.
2 Heat a frying pan and brush lightly with melted butter or oil. Stir the batter well and pour $^1/_4$ cup (60 ml/2 fl oz) into the pan, spreading with the back of a spoon. Cook until bubbles appear on the surface.
3 Turn the pancake over and cook the other side. Transfer to a plate and cover with a tea towel to keep warm while cooking the remaining batter. Arrange the pancakes in a stack, pile strawberries on top and drizzle with warm maple syrup.

COOK'S FILE

Variation: To make savoury polenta pancakes, simply remove the sugar from the batter. Serve with grilled tomatoes and breakfast sausages.

Cover the polenta with boiling water and stir until smooth.

Add the eggs to the polenta mixture and stir until smooth.

When bubbles appear on the surface, turn the pancake and cook the other side.

SPICY PANCAKES WITH CINNAMON CREAM

Preparation time: 20 minutes
+ 10 minutes standing
Total cooking time: 20–30 minutes
Makes about 12 pancakes

½ cup (60 g/2 oz) self-raising
    flour
½ cup (60 g/2 oz) plain
    flour
2 teaspoons mixed spice
½ teaspoon ground
    cardamom
1 tablespoon soft brown sugar
1 cup (250 ml/8 fl oz) milk
2 eggs
fresh raspberries, to serve

Cinnamon Cream
⅓ cup (90 g/3 oz) sour
    cream
2 tablespoons plain yoghurt
1 tablespoon honey or maple
    syrup
¼ teaspoon ground cinnamon

1 Sift the flours, spices and sugar into a large bowl and make a well in the centre. Mix the milk and eggs in a jug and pour into the well, whisking until just smooth. Cover with plastic wrap and leave for 10 minutes.
2 To make Cinnamon Cream: Mix all the ingredients together in a small bowl. Cover and refrigerate.
3 Heat a frying pan and brush lightly with melted butter or oil (use a non-stick pan if you have one). Add about 2 tablespoons batter to the pan, swirling gently to form a pancake about 12 cm (5 inches) in diameter. Cook over medium heat for about 1 minute, or until small bubbles begin to appear on the surface and the underside is golden. Turn over and cook the other side. Transfer to a plate and cover with a tea towel to keep warm while cooking the remaining batter. Serve warm with Cinnamon Cream, fresh raspberries and a light dusting of icing sugar.

Add the milk mixture to the well in the centre of the dry ingredients.

Make the Cinnamon Cream by mixing all the ingredients in a small bowl.

Add 2 tablespoons of the batter to the heated, greased pan.

BANANA BREAKFAST PANCAKES

Preparation time: 15 minutes
Total cooking time: 30 minutes
Makes 15 pancakes

 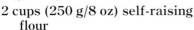

2 cups (250 g/8 oz) self-raising
flour
1/2 teaspoon ground nutmeg
1/4 cup (60 g/2 oz) caster sugar
2 eggs
1/2 cup (125 ml/4 fl oz) milk
1 cup (250 g/8 oz) light sour
cream

2 cups (480 g/15 1/3 oz) mashed
banana
125 g (4 oz) butter, whipped
maple syrup, to serve

1 Sift the flour and nutmeg into a large bowl and add the sugar. Whisk the eggs and milk together in a jug and add to the bowl with the sour cream and mashed banana. Stir until the batter is smooth.
2 Heat a frying pan and brush lightly with melted butter or oil. Pour about 1/4 cup (60 ml/2 fl oz) batter into the pan. Spread the batter gently to form a pancake about 10 cm (4 inches) in

diameter. Cook for about 2 minutes, or until bubbles appear on the surface.
3 Turn the pancake over and cook for 1–2 minutes, or until browned. Transfer to a plate and cover with a tea towel to keep warm while cooking the remaining batter. Top with a dollop of whipped butter and drizzle with maple syrup to serve.

COOK'S FILE

Note: To whip butter, let it come to room temperature then place it in a small bowl and beat with a wooden spoon or electric beaters until light and creamy.

Sift the self-raising flour and nutmeg together into a large bowl.

Add the milk mixture, sour cream and mashed banana.

Use the back of a spoon to gently spread the mixture in the pan.

PANETTONE PANCAKES WITH CHERRY BRANDY BUTTER

Preparation time: 25 minutes
Total cooking time: 15 minutes
Makes 11 pancakes

Cherry Brandy Butter
125 g (4 oz) unsalted butter, chopped
100 g (3⅓ oz) glacé cherries, finely chopped
2 tablespoons brandy

2 cups (250 g/8 oz) self-raising flour
150 g (4¾ oz) dried mixed fruit
1 tablespoon mixed peel
½ teaspoon ground nutmeg
4 eggs
⅓ cup (90 g/3 oz) caster sugar
1 cup (250 ml/8 fl oz) milk
1 cup (250 ml/8 fl oz) cream
30 g (1 oz) butter, melted

1 To make Cherry Brandy Butter: Place the butter, cherries and brandy in a food processor and process until well combined and almost smooth (don't worry if the mixture appears curdled). Set aside (refrigerate if the weather is warm).
2 Sift the flour into a large bowl. Add the dried fruit, mixed peel and nutmeg and make a well in the centre. Beat the eggs and sugar in a small bowl with electric beaters until thick and creamy and then stir in the milk, cream and butter. Gradually pour into the well, stirring until combined.
3 Heat a frying pan and brush lightly with melted butter or oil. Pour ¼ cup (60 ml/2 fl oz) batter into the pan, spreading out slightly to make a pancake. Cook over medium heat until lightly browned underneath.
4 Turn the pancake over and cook the other side. Transfer to a plate and cover with a tea towel to keep warm while cooking the remaining batter. Serve with Cherry Brandy Butter. Delicious topped with glacé cherries.

COOK'S FILE

Variation: Try glacé apricots, peaches, pineapple or ginger in place of the cherries in the butter, and use a complementary fruit liqueur.

Process the butter, glacé cherries and brandy until well combined.

Add the dried fruit, mixed peel and nutmeg to the flour.

Stir the milk, cream and butter into the combined eggs and sugar.

Pour the egg mixture into the dry ingredients and stir to combine.

Add the bicarbonate of soda to the dates and set aside to cool.

Stir the cooled date mixture through the combined flour and sugar.

Add the combined egg yolks and sour cream and stir until just smooth.

Beat the egg whites in a clean dry bowl until soft peaks form.

DATE PANCAKES WITH CARAMEL SAUCE

Preparation time: 35–40 minutes
Total cooking time: 30 minutes
Makes 10–12 pancakes

1 cup (185 g/6 oz) pitted and
  chopped dates
1 cup (250 ml/8 fl oz) water
1 teaspoon bicarbonate
  of soda
2 cups (250 g/8 oz) self-raising
  flour, sifted
1/2 cup (95 g/3¼ oz) soft brown
  sugar
1 cup (250 g/8 oz) sour cream
3 eggs, separated

Caramel Sauce
1 cup (185 g/6 oz) soft brown
  sugar
1 cup (250 ml/8 fl oz) cream
200 g (6½ oz) butter

1 Put the dates and water in a small pan and bring to the boil. Remove from the heat, stir in the bicarbonate of soda and cool for 5 minutes. Mix in a food processor until smooth. Cool.
2 Mix the flour and sugar in a large bowl. Stir in the date purée and make a well in the centre.
3 Whisk the sour cream and egg yolks together and pour into the well, stirring until the batter is just smooth. Beat the egg whites in a clean, dry bowl until soft peaks form. Stir a heaped tablespoon of egg white into the batter to loosen it, then fold in the remainder until just combined.
4 Heat a frying pan and brush lightly with melted butter or oil. Pour ¼ cup (60 ml/2 fl oz) batter into the pan. Cook for 2–3 minutes, or until bubbles form on the surface. Turn over and cook the other side. Remove and cover with a tea towel to keep warm while cooking the remaining batter. Serve with Caramel Sauce and ice cream.

5 To make Caramel Sauce: Stir the ingredients in a pan over medium heat, without boiling, until dissolved. Then simmer gently for 3–4 minutes.

SPINACH AND BRIE MOUNTAIN

Preparation time: 35 minutes
Total cooking time: 50 minutes
Serves 4–6

1 teaspoon baking powder
1/4 teaspoon salt
1 1/2 cups (185 g/6 oz) plain flour
2 eggs
2 1/2 cups (600 ml/20 fl oz) milk
60 g (2 oz) butter
3/4 cup (90 g/3 oz) grated
    Cheddar cheese
pinch of nutmeg
1 bunch (500 g/1 lb) English
    spinach
230 g (7 1/3 oz) Brie, chilled and
    thinly sliced
2 tomatoes, thinly sliced
2 tablespoons grated Parmesan

1 Sift the baking powder, salt and 1 cup (125 g/4 oz) flour into a large bowl and make a well in the centre. Whisk the eggs and half the milk in a jug and pour into the well, whisking until just combined.

2 Heat a frying pan and brush lightly with melted butter or oil. Pour 1/4 cup (60 ml/2 fl oz) batter into the pan and cook until small bubbles form on the surface and the underside is brown. Turn over and cook the other side. Remove and cover with a tea towel while you cook the rest of the batter.

3 Melt the butter in a saucepan, stir in the remaining flour and cook for 2 minutes. Add the remaining milk and stir until the mixture boils and thickens. Stir in the cheese, nutmeg and salt and cracked pepper, to taste. Remove from the heat once the cheese has melted and the sauce is smooth.

4 Preheat the oven to moderately hot 200°C (400°F/Gas 6). Trim the spinach and wash well. Place in a pan with just the water clinging to the leaves and steam until wilted. Cool slightly and use your hands to squeeze out any liquid. Tear the spinach into pieces.

5 Layer the pancakes, spinach, sliced Brie and tomato in a round ovenproof dish, finishing with a pancake. Spread the cheese sauce over the top, making sure it covers the sides. Sprinkle with Parmesan cheese. Bake for 25–30 minutes and serve cut into thick wedges.

Make a well in the centre of the dry ingredients and whisk in the milk mixture.

Stir the cheese, nutmeg, salt and cracked pepper into the sauce.

Place the washed spinach in a pan, cover and steam until the leaves are wilted.

BEAN WEDGES WITH SALSA AND GUACAMOLE

Preparation time: 20 minutes
Total cooking time: 30 minutes
Serves 4

2 cups (250 g/8 oz) self-raising
    flour
2 cups (500 ml/16 fl oz)
    buttermilk
2 eggs
60 g (2 oz) butter, melted
290 g (9½ oz) can red kidney
    beans, drained

Salsa
4 large tomatoes, finely chopped
1 small red onion, finely
    chopped
2 small red chillies, finely
    chopped
1 tablespoon chopped fresh
    coriander
½ green capsicum, finely
    chopped

Guacamole
1 large avocado
2 teaspoons lemon juice
1 teaspoon chilli sauce
2 tablespoons sour cream
½ cup (60 g/2 oz) grated
    Cheddar cheese

1 Preheat the oven to moderately hot 200°C (400°F/Gas 6). Put the flour, buttermilk, eggs and butter in a food processor and process for 10 seconds, or until smooth. Transfer to a bowl and fold in the beans.
2 Heat a small non-stick frying pan and brush lightly with melted butter or oil. Pour ¼ cup (60 ml/2 fl oz) batter over the base of the pan and cook over medium heat until golden brown. Turn over and cook the other side. Remove and cover while you cook the remaining batter. Cut each pancake into thin wedges. Brush the wedges lightly with oil and place on a non-stick baking tray. Bake for 15 minutes, or until edges are crisp.

3 To make Salsa: Mix together all the ingredients and refrigerate.
4 To make Guacamole: Mash the avocado in a bowl until smooth. Mix in the lemon juice, chilli sauce and sour cream. Serve bean wedges and Salsa, topped with Guacamole and sprinkled with Cheddar cheese.

Use a metal spoon to gently fold the kidney beans through the batter.

When all the pancakes are cooked, cut them into thin wedges.

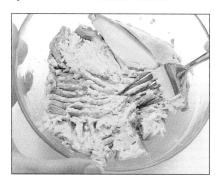

Use a fork to mash the peeled avocado in a bowl until smooth.

CRISPY CRAB PANCAKES

Preparation time: 25 minutes
Total cooking time: 25 minutes
Makes 8

1 teaspoon baking powder
1 cup (125 g/4 oz) plain flour
1/4 teaspoon salt
2 eggs
1 1/3 cups (350 ml/11 fl oz) milk

Filling
345 g (11 oz) fresh or well-
    drained canned crab meat
1 egg, beaten
1/4 teaspoon salt
2 tablespoons cornflour
2 tablespoons coconut cream
2 tablespoons chopped fresh
    coriander
1/2 cup (45 g/1 1/2 oz) bean
    sprouts
beaten egg, to glaze

Coating
1 egg, beaten
2 tablespoons milk
plain flour
2/3 cup (65 g/2 1/4 oz) dry
    breadcrumbs
oil for deep-frying

1 Sift the baking powder, flour and salt into a large bowl and make a well in the centre. Whisk the eggs and milk in a jug and pour into the well, whisking until just smooth. Heat a frying pan and brush with melted butter. Pour 1/4 cup (60 ml/2 fl oz) batter into the pan. Cook over medium heat until the underside is golden. Turn over and cook the other side. Remove and cover with a tea towel while cooking the remaining batter.

2 To make Filling: Mix together the crab meat, egg, salt, cornflour, coconut cream, coriander and bean sprouts. Place equal amounts of filling in the middle of each pancake, turn in the edges and roll up tightly to make a parcel. Brush the edge with beaten egg to seal.

3 For Coating: Beat together the egg and milk. Coat the parcels lightly with flour, then dip into the egg mixture and roll in the breadcrumbs. Heat the oil to moderately hot and deep-fry the parcels, one or two at a time, until golden and crisp. Drain on paper towels. Serve at once with wedges of lemon or lime.

COOK'S FILE

Note: To prepare in advance, coat the parcels in the breadcrumbs, then cover and refrigerate until ready to deep-fry.

Hint: To make the pancakes easy to roll you may need to thin the batter with a little milk.

Whisk the egg mixture into the dry ingredients until just smooth.

Roll up the filled pancakes tightly, turning in the edges to form a parcel.

Coat the parcels with flour, then the egg mixture, then roll in the breadcrumbs.

Cook the eggplant in batches over high heat until the pieces are golden brown.

Fold the cooled eggplant and shredded basil through the batter.

When the sweet potato is very soft, remove the cinnamon stick.

Pour 1/4 cup eggplant batter into the greased and heated frying pan.

EGGPLANT PANCAKES WITH SWEET POTATO MASH

Preparation time: 40 minutes
Total cooking time: 20 minutes
  + 20 minutes standing
Serves 4

1 large eggplant, diced
    (about 450 g/14¹/₃ oz)
¹/₄ cup (60 ml/2 fl oz) olive oil
¹/₃ cup (50 g/1²/₃ oz) polenta
¹/₂ cup (60 g/2 oz) plain flour
¹/₄ teaspoon baking powder
2 teaspoons grated lime rind
1 cup (250 ml/8 fl oz) milk
2 eggs
2 tablespoons shredded basil

Sweet Potato Mash
30 g (1 oz) butter
1 tablespoon grated fresh ginger
1 onion, finely chopped
500 g (1 lb) orange sweet
    potato, diced
3 tablespoons orange juice
1 cinnamon stick
1 cup (250 g/8 oz) fresh ricotta

1 Sprinkle the eggplant liberally with salt, then drain in a colander for about 20 minutes. Rinse and pat dry with paper towels. Heat the oil in a frying pan and brown the eggplant in batches over high heat. Drain on paper towels and set aside to cool.

2 Sift the polenta, flour and baking powder into a bowl and make a well in the centre. Whisk the lime rind, milk and eggs together in a jug and pour into the well, whisking until just combined. Fold the eggplant and basil through the batter.

3 To make Sweet Potato Mash: Melt the butter in a pan. Add the ginger and onion and cook over medium heat for 3 minutes, or until golden. Add the sweet potato and cook until beginning to soften. Add the orange juice and cinnamon stick; cover and simmer until the sweet potato is very soft. Remove the cinnamon. Mash the sweet potato until smooth. Mix in the ricotta.

4 Heat a lightly oiled frying pan and add ¹/₄ cup (60 ml/2 fl oz) batter. Cook over medium heat for 2 minutes, or until the underside is golden. Turn and cook the other side until golden. Remove and cover while cooking the remaining batter. Serve with Sweet Potato Mash.

PANCAKES, PIKELETS, CREPES AND WAFFLES

CHICKEN PANCAKES WITH CHAR-GRILLED VEGETABLES AND FETA

Preparation time: 40 minutes
  + 30 minutes marinating
Total cooking time: 30 minutes
Serves 4

Char-grilled Vegetables
1 red capsicum, thickly sliced
1 yellow capsicum, thickly
    sliced
1 kg (2 lb) baby bok choy,
    leaves, separated
2 zucchini, cut into strips
8 small field mushrooms
1/4 cup (60 ml/2 fl oz) Italian
    salad dressing

1/2 cup (60 g/2 oz) plain flour
pinch of salt
1 1/3 cups (350 ml/11 fl oz)
    buttermilk
2 eggs
1 teaspoon oil
2 smoked chicken breasts,
    thinly sliced
150 g (4 3/4 oz) Bulgarian feta
olive oil, to serve

1 **To prepare Char-grilled Vegetables:** Put the vegetables in a small bowl with the dressing and marinate for at least 30 minutes.
2 Sift the flour and salt into a bowl and make a well in the centre. Whisk the buttermilk, eggs and oil in a jug and pour into the well, whisking until just combined. Add the sliced smoked chicken and mix gently to combine.
3 Heat a small crepe or non-stick frying pan and brush lightly with melted butter or oil. Pour 1/4 cup (60 ml/2 fl oz) batter into the pan, quickly spreading the chicken to ensure it is evenly distributed. Cook over medium heat for 2 minutes, or until the underside is golden. Turn over and cook the other side. Transfer to a plate and cover while cooking the remaining batter. Cut each pancake into wedges.

4 Cook the vegetables on a hot barbecue or char-grill plate for 3 minutes, or until tender. Divide the vegetables among four plates and top with the pancake wedges and a little crumbled feta. Drizzle with olive oil and sprinkle with cracked black pepper to serve.

Carefully separate the leaves of the baby bok choy.

Add the slices of smoked chicken to the batter and mix gently to combine.

Quickly spread the chicken out so that it is evenly distributed through the pancake.

CHIVE PANCAKES WITH SMOKED TROUT CREAM

Preparation time: 15 minutes
Total cooking time: 10 minutes
Makes 6

Smoked Trout Cream
250 g (8 oz) smoked trout, skin
   and bones removed
150 g (4³/4 oz) soft cream cheese
¹/2 cup (125 g/4 oz) sour cream
2 spring onions, finely chopped
1 tablespoon lemon or lime juice

1 cup (125 g/4 oz) plain flour
1 teaspoon sugar
1 teaspoon finely grated lemon
   or lime rind
1 egg
20 g (²/3 oz) butter, melted
1 cup (250 ml/8 fl oz) water
¹/4 cup (15 g/¹/2 oz) snipped fresh
   chives

1 To make Smoked Trout Cream: Set aside 6 small pieces of smoked trout to garnish. Place the remaining smoked trout, cream cheese, sour cream, spring onions and juice in a bowl and beat until smooth. Add some cracked black pepper, to taste, and set aside.
2 Place the flour, sugar and rind into a food processor and process briefly to combine. With the machine running, gradually add the combined egg, butter and water, processing until the mixture is free of lumps. Transfer to a bowl and gently fold in the chives.
3 Heat a crepe or non-stick frying pan and brush lightly with melted butter or oil. Add ¹/4 cup (60 ml/2 fl oz) batter to the pan, swirling gently to coat the base. Cook the pancake for 1 minute, or until the underside is golden. Turn over and cook the other side. Transfer to a plate and cover with a tea towel to keep warm while cooking the remaining batter.
4 Divide the smoked trout mixture among the pancakes and fold up into parcels. Garnish with the reserved trout and serve with lime wedges.

COOK'S FILE

Hint: The trout filling mixture can be prepared up to 1 hour before serving. Cover and keep refrigerated.

Use a knife to remove the skin and bones from the trout.

Combine the trout, cream cheese, sour cream, spring onions and juice.

With the motor running, gradually add the egg mixture to the processor.

Divide the filling among the pancakes and then fold up into parcels.

PEKING DUCK PARCELS

Preparation time: 40 minutes
  + 30 minutes standing
Total cooking time: 15–20 minutes
Makes 12 parcels

1 cup (125 g/4 oz) plain flour
¹/4 cup (30 g/1 oz) cornflour
3 eggs
²/3 cup (170 ml/5¹/2 fl oz) milk
²/3 cup (170 ml/5¹/2 fl oz) water
30 g (1 oz) butter, melted
4 spring onions, finely chopped
1 Chinese barbecued duck
2 carrots, cut into julienne
  strips (see note)
1 celery stalk, cut into julienne
  strips
6 spring onions, cut into
  julienne strips
1 lebanese cucumber, cut into
  julienne strips
hoisin sauce

1 Place the flour, cornflour, eggs, milk, water and butter in a food processor. Process for 15–20 seconds, or until combined and smooth. Pour the batter into a jug, cover and set aside for 30 minutes.

2 Heat a medium-sized crepe pan or non-stick frying pan and brush with melted butter or oil. Pour about ¹/4 cup (60 ml/2 fl oz) batter into the pan and swirl quickly to cover the base; pour off the excess into a jug (take care not to make the pancakes too thin).

3 Quickly sprinkle the pancake with some chopped spring onion. Cook for about 30 seconds, then turn the pancake over and cook the other side. Transfer to a plate and cover with a tea towel to keep warm while cooking the remaining batter.

4 Strip the meat and some crispy skin from the duck. Shred and divide the meat into 12 portions and set aside with the skin. Blanch the carrots and celery in a pan of boiling water for 2 minutes. Drain and cool quickly in cold water, then drain on paper towels. Combine the julienned carrot, celery, spring onion and cucumber and divide into 12 portions.

5 Place a pancake, spring onion side up, on a board. Fold under the top one-third of the pancake. Spread the remaining two-thirds of the pancake with about 1 teaspoon of hoisin sauce. Arrange a portion of duck meat and some of the crispy skin on the centre of the pancake, leaving the lower one-third uncovered.

6 Arrange the julienned vegetables on top of the duck, extending them decoratively over the top fold of the pancake. Fold in the base and sides to form a firm parcel. Seal with a little extra hoisin sauce. Repeat with the remaining pancakes and filling.

COOK'S FILE

Note: Julienne strips are long thin strips of vegetables cut with a sharp knife to about the width of a matchstick. They cook quickly, usually requiring just a quick blanching in boiling water, and look very attractive.

Variation: Chinese barbecue ducks, also known as Peking Ducks, are bought from Chinese butchers, but if they aren't available, use barbecued Chinese pork, cut into strips.

Note: The vegetables are a matter of personal choice. Add bean sprouts or sliced bean shoots if you prefer.

Cut the carrots, celery, spring onions and cucumber into julienne strips.

Swirl the batter over the base of the pan— don't make the pancakes too thin.

Sprinkle the uncooked pancakes with some chopped spring onion.

Strip the meat and some of the crispy skin from the duck.

Spread some hoisin sauce over the remaining two-thirds of the pancake.

Fold in the base and sides of the pancake to form a parcel.

SPICED PANCAKES WITH BEETROOT SALAD AND GOATS CHEESE

Preparation time: 20 minutes
+ 20 minutes standing
Total cooking time: 30 minutes
Serves 4

1/2 cup (60 g/2 oz) self-raising
　flour
1/2 cup (75 g/21/2 oz) wholemeal
　plain flour
1/2 teaspoon ground cumin
1/2 teaspoon ground coriander
1/2 teaspoon ground cinnamon
2 teaspoons grated orange rind
1 cup (250 ml/8 fl oz) milk
2 eggs
100 g (31/3 oz) goats cheese

Beetroot Salad
1 bunch baby beetroot, stems
　removed leaving 2 cm
　(3/4 inch) stalk attached
1 red onion, cut into thin
　wedges
1 teaspoon sugar
2 tablespoons balsamic vinegar
2 tablespoons chopped mint

1 Sift the flours and spices into a bowl. Stir in the orange rind and make a well in the centre. Whisk the milk and eggs in a jug and pour into the well, whisking to just combine. Cover and set aside for 20 minutes.
2 To make Beetroot Salad: Cook the beetroot in boiling water for 15 minutes, or until tender. Remove the skins and cut the flesh into wedges. Place the beetroot, red onion, sugar and balsamic vinegar in a bowl and mix to combine. Refrigerate.
3 Heat a frying pan and brush lightly

with melted butter or oil. Spoon 2 tablespoons of the batter into the pan. Cook over medium heat for 1 minute, or until the underside is golden. Turn over and cook the other side. Remove and cover with a tea towel while cooking the remaining batter. Stack the pancakes on plates, top with slices of goats cheese and sprinkle with cracked black pepper. Fold the chopped mint through the salad and serve with the pancakes.

Make a well in the dry ingredients, add the milk mixture and whisk to a batter.

Use your fingers to remove the skins from the cooked beetroot.

When the underside is golden, flip the pancake over and cook the other side.

BAKED CHICKEN AND ARTICHOKE PANCAKES

Preparation time: 30 minutes
Total cooking time: 1 hour
Serves 4

1 teaspoon baking powder
1$\frac{1}{3}$ cups (165 g/5$\frac{1}{2}$ oz) plain
   flour
$\frac{1}{4}$ teaspoon salt
2 eggs
300 ml (9$\frac{2}{3}$ fl oz) milk
90 g (3 oz) butter
2$\frac{1}{2}$ cups (600 ml/20 fl oz)
   chicken stock
2 egg yolks
1 cup (250 ml/8 fl oz) cream
1 teaspoon lemon juice
300 g (9$\frac{2}{3}$ oz) cooked chicken,
   chopped roughly
350 g (11$\frac{1}{4}$ oz) artichoke
   hearts, drained and sliced
2 teaspoons chopped thyme
2 teaspoons chopped parsley
100 g (3$\frac{1}{3}$ oz) Parmesan,
   freshly grated

1 Sift the baking powder, 1 cup (125 g/4 oz) flour and salt into a large bowl and make a well in the centre. Whisk the eggs and milk in a jug and pour into the well, whisking until just smooth. Heat a frying pan and brush lightly with melted butter. Add $\frac{1}{4}$ cup (60 ml/2 fl oz) batter and cook over medium heat until the underside is brown. Turn over and cook the other side. Transfer to a plate and cover with a tea towel while cooking the remaining batter.
2 Melt the butter in a pan and stir in the remaining flour. Cook for 2 minutes, then remove from the heat. Slowly whisk in the chicken stock until smooth. Whisk in the combined yolks and cream. Return to the heat and bring slowly to the boil, stirring continuously. Boil for 30 seconds to thicken the sauce, then remove from the heat and stir in the lemon juice. Add salt and freshly ground black pepper, to taste.
3 Preheat the oven to moderately hot 200°C (400°F/Gas 6). Grease a 3-litre capacity ovenproof dish with melted butter. Line the base with 2 pancakes, slightly overlapping. Divide the chicken, artichokes and herbs in half. Spoon one half evenly over the pancakes. Pour a third of the sauce over the top and layer with another two pancakes. Repeat, finishing with a layer of 3 pancakes. Spread the final third of the sauce over the top, sprinkle with Parmesan and bake for 30–35 minutes, or until golden brown.

Heat a frying pan and pour in $\frac{1}{4}$ cup (60 ml/2 fl oz) batter for each pancake.

Slowly whisk in the combined yolks and cream, away from the heat.

Line the dish with pancakes, then spoon in half the chicken and artichoke filling.

PIKELETS

PIKELETS WITH JAM AND CREAM

Preparation time: 15 minutes
Total cooking time: 10 minutes
Makes 18

1 cup (125 g/4 oz) self-raising
    flour
pinch of salt
1 tablespoon caster sugar
3/4 cup (185 ml/6 fl oz) milk
1 egg
jam and freshly whipped cream,
    to serve

1 Sift the flour, salt and sugar into a large bowl and make a well in the centre. Whisk the milk and egg in a jug and slowly pour into the well, whisking to form a smooth batter.

2 Heat a frying pan (a non-stick pan is best, if you have one) and brush lightly with melted butter or oil.
3 Drop level tablespoonsful of the batter into the frying pan, allowing room for spreading (you will probably fit about four pikelets in the pan at a time). Cook the pikelets over moderate heat for about 30 seconds, or until small bubbles begin to appear on the surface and the underneath has turned golden brown.
4 Turn the pikelets over and cook the other side. Transfer to a plate or wire rack to cool. Repeat the process with the remaining batter. Serve the pikelets topped with jam and freshly whipped cream.

COOK'S FILE

Note: Delicious served with a little poached fruit.

Gradually pour the milk mixture into the well in the centre of the dry ingredients.

Brush the heated pan lightly with melted butter or oil.

Drop level tablespoonsful of batter into the pan, allowing room for spreading.

When bubbles form on the surface, flip the pikelets over and cook the other side.

APPLE AND BUTTERMILK PIKELETS WITH CINNAMON SUGAR

Preparation time: 15 minutes
Total cooking time: 15 minutes
Makes about 12

1 egg
1 cup (250 ml/8 fl oz)
    buttermilk
1/2 cup (125 g/4 oz) caster sugar
30 g (1 oz) butter, melted
1 small green apple, peeled,
    cored and grated
1 cup (125 g/4 oz) plain flour
1/2 teaspoon bicarbonate of soda
1 teaspoon ground cinnamon

1 Combine the egg, buttermilk, 2 tablespoons of caster sugar and the melted butter in a bowl and beat until smooth. Stir in the grated apple.
2 Sift the flour and bicarbonate of soda into a bowl and make a well in the centre. Pour the buttermilk mixture into the well. Stir until the mixture is just moistened, taking care not to overbeat.
3 Melt a little butter in a frying pan and then add 2 heaped tablespoons of the batter to make each pikelet, leaving room for spreading (you will probably fit 3–4 pikelets in the pan). Cook for 2–3 minutes, or until small bubbles appear on the surface and the underside is golden brown. Turn over and cook for 1–2 minutes, or until lightly golden brown. Transfer to a plate and cover with a tea towel to keep warm while cooking the rest of the batter. Combine the remaining caster sugar with the cinnamon and sprinkle over the pikelets. Delicious with mascarpone and blueberries.

Stir the grated apple into the combined egg, buttermilk, sugar and butter.

Using a wooden spoon, stir until the mixture is just moistened.

Use 2 heaped tablespoons of batter to make each pikelet.

CURRANT AND LEMON PIKELETS

Preparation time: 10–15 minutes
Total cooking time: 15 minutes
Makes about 12

1 cup (125 g/4 oz) self-raising flour
1/4 teaspoon bicarbonate of soda
2 tablespoons caster sugar
1/2 cup (75 g/2 1/2 oz) currants
1 teaspoon grated lemon rind
1 teaspoon vinegar
3/4 cup (185 ml/6 fl oz) milk
1 egg
20 g (2/3 oz) butter, melted

1 Sift the flour and bicarbonate of soda into a bowl. Stir in the caster sugar, currants and lemon rind and make a well in the centre. Combine the vinegar and milk in a small jug and whisk into the well with the egg and melted butter.

2 Stir to form a thick smooth batter. Melt a little butter in a frying pan (non-stick is best, if you have one) and drop slightly heaped tablespoons of batter into the pan, leaving room for the pikelets to spread.

3 Cook for 2 minutes, or until bubbles appear on the surface, then turn over and cook the other side until lightly browned. Transfer to a plate and cover with a tea towel to keep warm while cooking the remaining batter. Spread with butter and jam to serve.

Stir the caster sugar, currants and lemon rind into the sifted flour.

Whisk the milk mixture, egg and melted butter into the dry ingredients.

Cook the pikelets for about 2 minutes, or until bubbles appear on the surface.

RICOTTA PIKELETS WITH ROASTED WALNUTS AND MAPLE SYRUP

Preparation time: 10–15 minutes
Total cooking time: 15 minutes
Makes about 10

3/4 cup (90 g/3 oz) walnut pieces
3 eggs
2 tablespoons caster sugar
250 g (8 oz) ricotta
1 teaspoon grated lemon rind
1/4 cup (30 g/1 oz) plain flour,
    sifted
50 g (1²/3 oz) butter, melted
maple syrup, to serve
strawberries, to serve

1 Place the walnuts on a foil-lined tray and roast under a preheated grill for 1–2 minutes, or until golden. Cool and chop finely.

2 Whisk together the eggs and sugar in a bowl. Add the ricotta and lemon rind and beat until smooth.

3 Add the flour all at once to the bowl and then pour the butter down the side of the bowl; stir both into the mixture until just combined, taking care not to overbeat.

4 Heat a frying pan and brush lightly with melted butter. Add heaped tablespoonsful of the batter to the pan and spread out to circles of about 6 cm (2¹/2 inches) in diameter, leaving a little room for further spreading. Cook for 2–3 minutes, or until small bubbles begin to appear on the surface and the pikelets look partially firm. Turn the pikelets over and cook the other side until light golden brown. Transfer to a plate and cover with a tea towel to keep warm while cooking the rest of the batter. Serve the pikelets with warmed maple syrup and a sprinkling of roasted chopped walnuts and fresh strawberries.

COOK'S FILE

Note: Any type of nut can be used for this recipe as well as walnuts. Hazelnuts, macadamias, pecans or almonds would all be suitable. Roasting the nuts develops the flavour and makes removing the skin easier. Place the roasted nuts in a clean dry tea towel and rub gently to remove the skins.

Lightly toast the walnuts on a foil-lined tray under a preheated grill.

Add the flour all at once and then pour the butter down the side of the bowl.

Add the ricotta cheese to the combined eggs and sugar mixture.

Spread the mixture to form circles (you should be able to fit 3 or 4 in your pan).

Stir the coffee powder, sugar and Kahlua over low heat until the sugar dissolves.

Gradually stir the cooled Kahlua mixture into the whipped cream.

Gradually whisk the egg mixture into the dry ingredients until just smooth.

Cook until small bubbles appear on the surface and the underside has coloured.

CAPPUCCINO PIKELETS WITH KAHLUA CREAM

Preparation time: 25 minutes
Total cooking time: 20 minutes
Makes 15–20

Kahlua Cream
2 teaspoons espresso coffee powder
2 tablespoons caster sugar
1/4 cup (60 ml/2 fl oz) Kahlua
300 ml (9²/3 fl oz) cream, lightly whipped

1/4 cup (60 ml/2 fl oz) boiling water
1 tablespoon espresso coffee powder
1/4 teaspoon ground cinnamon
2 cups (250 g/8 oz) self-raising flour
1/2 cup (95 g/3¹/4 oz) soft brown sugar
2 eggs
1 cup (250 ml/8 fl oz) milk
fresh strawberries, to serve

1 To make Kahlua Cream: Combine the coffee powder, sugar and Kahlua in a small pan. Stir over low heat until the sugar dissolves. Set aside to cool, then gradually stir into the cream until smooth. Cover and refrigerate until ready to serve.

2 Pour boiling water over the coffee powder and cinnamon in a bowl; stir to dissolve and set aside to cool.

3 Sift the flour into a bowl and stir in the sugar, making a well in the centre. Whisk the eggs, milk and cooled coffee in a jug and gradually pour into the well, whisking until just smooth. Heat a frying pan and brush lightly with melted butter or oil. Drop heaped tablespoons of batter into the pan, allowing room for spreading.

4 Cook the pikelets over moderate heat until small bubbles appear on the surface and the underside has coloured. Turn over and cook the other side. Transfer to a plate and cover with a tea towel to keep warm while cooking the remaining batter. Serve with strawberries and Kahlua Cream sprinkled with cocoa powder.

COOK'S FILE

Note: You can use instant coffee powder but the flavour will not be as strong as with the espresso powder.

GLAZED FRUIT PIKELETS

Preparation time: 25 minutes
Total cooking time: 15 minutes
Makes about 15

1 cup (125 g/4 oz) self-raising
    flour
2 tablespoons caster sugar
1 egg
3/4 cup (185 ml/6 fl oz) milk
100 g (3 1/3 oz) cream cheese,
    softened
strawberries and kiwi fruit

3 tablespoons strawberry jam
squeeze of fresh lemon juice

1 Sift the flour into a bowl and mix in the sugar; make a well in the centre. Whisk the egg and milk in a jug and pour into the well, whisking until just combined. Do not overmix.
2 Heat a frying pan and brush lightly with melted butter or oil. Drop tablespoonsful of the mixture into the pan, allowing room for spreading. Cook over medium heat for 30 seconds, or until small bubbles begin to appear on the surface and the underside turns golden brown. Turn over and cook the other side until golden. Place on a wire rack to cool while cooking the remaining batter.
3 Once cool, spread generously with cream cheese and arrange sliced strawberries and kiwi fruit on top. Gently heat the strawberry jam, add a squeeze of lemon juice and stir to combine. Brush over the fruit to glaze.

COOK'S FILE

Note: For a sweeter and creamier taste, use mascarpone instead of cream cheese.

Sift the flour into a bowl and then mix in the sugar.

Drop tablespoonsful of the batter into the heated pan.

Add a squeeze of lemon juice to the heated jam to make a glaze.

Stir the rice and melted butter into the combined milk, egg yolks and sugar.

Add the sifted flour and stir until the mixture is just moistened.

Gently fold the beaten egg whites into the rice mixture, taking care not to overmix.

RICE GRIDDLECAKES WITH STEWED FRUIT

Preparation time: 15 minutes
Total cooking time: 15 minutes
Makes about 15

1 cup (250 ml/8 fl oz) milk
2 eggs, separated
1 tablespoon caster sugar
1 cup (185 g/6 oz) cooked rice
20 g (²/3 oz) butter, melted
1 cup (125 g/4 oz) plain flour, sifted
stewed fruit, for serving

1 Whisk the milk, egg yolks and caster sugar together in a bowl. Stir in the rice and melted butter.
2 Add the sifted flour to the bowl all at once and stir until the ingredients are just moistened.
3 Place the egg whites in a small clean dry bowl and beat until firm peaks form. Gently fold into the rice mixture, taking care not to overmix.
4 Heat a frying pan and brush lightly with melted butter or oil. Add 2 tablespoons of the rice mixture to the pan and spread to a circle about 8 cm (3 inches) in diameter. Cook for 2–3 minutes, or until small bubbles appear on the surface and the mixture looks partially firm. Turn the griddlecake over and cook the other side for 1–2 minutes, or until lightly browned. Transfer to a plate and cover with a tea towel to keep warm while you cook the remaining batter. Serve with stewed fruit and perhaps dust with a little icing sugar.

Add 2 tablespoons of the prepared rice mixture to the pan.

COOK'S FILE

Note: About ¹/3 cup (75 g/2¹/2 oz) of raw rice will produce 1 cup of rice when cooked.

BOOZY FRUIT PIKELETS

Preparation time: 15 minutes
+ 4 hours soaking
Total cooking time: 15 minutes
Makes 25–30

150 g (4³/4 oz) blueberries
150 g (4³/4 oz) raspberries
¹/3 cup (80 ml/2³/4 fl oz)
    blackcurrant liqueur
1 cup (125 g/4 oz) self-raising
    flour
¹/4 teaspoon salt
1 egg
¹/4 cup (60 g/2 oz) sugar

Sift the flour and salt into a bowl before making a well in the centre.

³/4 cup (185 ml/6 fl oz) milk
25 g (³/4 oz) butter, melted
150 g (4³/4 oz) mascarpone

1 Gently combine the blueberries, raspberries and liqueur in a bowl. Cover and refrigerate for 4 hours, stirring gently two or three times, or leave overnight.
2 Sift the flour and salt into a bowl and make a well in the centre.
3 Beat together the egg and sugar until thick, then beat in the milk. Pour into the well with the melted butter, whisking until just smooth.
4 Heat a frying pan (use a non-stick pan if you have one) and brush lightly

Using a wooden spoon, make a well in the centre of the dry ingredients.

with melted butter or oil. Drop tablespoonsful of the batter into the pan, allowing a little room for spreading. Cook the pikelets over moderate heat until bubbles begin to appear on the surface and the undersides are golden brown. Turn the pikelets over and cook the other sides. Remove from the pan; cool on a wire rack while cooking the remaining batter. Spread mascarpone generously onto each pikelet and top with the fruit. Drizzle lightly with the liqueur just before serving.

C O O K ' S   F I L E

Note: Use canned, if fresh berries aren't available, but drain them well.

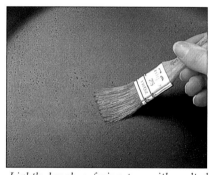

Lightly brush a frying pan with melted butter or oil.

BLUEBERRY PIKELETS

Preparation time: 15 minutes
Total cooking time: 20 minutes
Makes about 24

1 cup (125 g/4 oz) self-raising
    flour
2 tablespoons caster sugar
1 egg
20 g (²/3 oz) butter, melted
1 teaspoon vanilla essence

Combine the egg, butter, vanilla essence and milk together in a jug.

³/4 cup (185 ml/6 fl oz) milk
150 g (4³/4 oz) fresh blueberries

1 Sift the flour into a bowl and stir in the caster sugar. Make a well in the centre of the mixture.
2 Whisk together the egg, butter, vanilla essence and milk in a jug and pour into the well, whisking until just combined. Do not overmix. Gently stir in the blueberries.
3 Heat a frying pan and brush lightly with melted butter or oil. Pour table-

Add the blueberries to the batter and gently stir in until just combined.

spoonsful of the batter into the pan, leaving a little room for spreading, and cook until bubbles appear on the surface. Turn over and cook the other side until lightly browned. Remove from the pan and keep warm while cooking the remainder. Serve hot with maple syrup or honey, if liked.

C O O K ' S   F I L E

Hint: Keep the pikelets warm under a tea towel or in a preheated slow 150°C (300°F/Gas 2) oven.

Cook the pikelets until bubbles appear on the surface, then turn over.

*Boozy Fruit Pikelets (top)
and Blueberry Pikelets*

CINNAMON APPLE PIKELETS

Preparation time: 30 minutes
Total cooking time: 15–20 minutes
Makes 25–30

1 cup (125 g/4 oz) plain flour
1 teaspoon baking powder
1/4 teaspoon salt
1 egg
1/4 cup (60 g/2 oz) caster sugar

3/4 cup (185 ml/6 fl oz) milk
25 g (3/4 oz) butter, melted
2 apples
1 tablespoon lemon juice
soft brown sugar

1 Sift the flour, baking powder and salt into a large bowl and make a well in the centre. Beat the egg and sugar in a jug until thick, then add the milk and melted butter. Pour into the well, whisking until just smooth.

2 Peel, core and quarter the apples. Thinly slice and sprinkle with the lemon juice to prevent browning.

3 Heat a frying pan and brush lightly with melted butter or oil. Add heaped tablespoons of the batter to the pan. Place 3 slices of apple onto each pikelet and cook until the underside is golden. Sprinkle with a little sugar. Turn over and cook the other side until golden. Keep warm while you cook the rest of the batter. Serve hot with whipped cream and a dusting of ground cinnamon, if preferred.

Gradually whisk the milk mixture into the dry ingredients until just smooth.

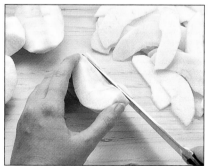

Peel and core the apples, then sprinkle with lemon juice to prevent browning.

Place 3 slices of apple on top of each pikelet in the pan.

ORANGE AND POPPY SEED PIKELETS

Preparation time: 15 minutes
Total cooking time: 20 minutes
Makes about 20

2 cups (250 g/8 oz) self-raising
  flour
1/4 cup (60 g/2 oz) caster sugar
2 tablespoons poppy seeds
1 tablespoon grated orange rind

2 eggs
1/2 cup (125 g/4 oz) sour cream
3/4 cup (185 ml/6 fl oz) milk

1 Sift the flour into a bowl. Stir in the the sugar, poppy seeds and the orange rind. Make a well in the centre. Whisk together the eggs, sour cream and milk in a small jug and pour into the well, whisking until just smooth. Add more milk, if necessary, until the batter has a pouring consistency.

2 Heat a frying pan (use a non-stick pan if you have one) and brush lightly with melted butter. Drop heaped tablespoonsful of the batter into the pan, allowing a little room for spreading. Cook the pikelets over moderate heat until bubbles appear on the surface and the underside is golden.

3 Turn the pikelets over and cook the other side. Transfer to a plate and cover with a tea towel to keep warm while you cook the remaining batter. Serve warm—delicious with plenty of butter and honey.

Stir the sugar, poppy seeds and orange rind into the sifted flour.

Drop heaped tablespoonsful of the mixture into the heated pan.

When the underside is golden brown, turn over and cook the other side.

39

COCKTAIL BLINIS

Blinis are excellent for fuss-free entertaining—they look stunningly professional but are really very easy to make and can be prepared well ahead of time. Use the toppings suggested below or whip up some ideas of your own.

BASIC BLINI METHOD

Sift ³/4 cup (90 g/3 oz) self-raising flour, ¹/4 teaspoon bicarbonate of soda and a pinch of salt into a bowl and make a well in the centre. Combine 1 teaspoon grated lemon rind, ¹/3 cup (80 ml/2³/4 fl oz) milk, ¹/3 cup (90 g/3 oz) sour cream and 1 egg in a jug and pour into the well, whisking until the mixture is just smooth. Cover the bowl with plastic wrap and set aside for about 10 minutes. Heat a frying pan and brush lightly with melted butter or oil. Drop heaped teaspoons of the batter into the pan, allowing room for spreading. Cook the blinis for about 30 seconds, or until small bubbles begin to appear on the surface and the underside is golden brown. Turn the blinis over and cook the other side. Transfer to a plate or wire rack to cool while cooking the remaining batter. When all the blinis are cooked, top with a selection of the following toppings. Makes about 30.

BOCCONCINI AND TOMATO

Place a thin slice of bocconcini and egg tomato on the top of each blini. Top with a basil leaf and a little freshly ground black pepper.

SAUTEED VEGETABLE
WITH GARLIC MAYONNAISE

Finely dice 1 small red capsicum, 1 onion and 1 tomato. Heat a little olive oil in a frying pan. Add the onion and cook for 1 minute. Stir in the capsicum and tomato. Cook over medium heat for 2–3 minutes to soften and reduce any liquid. Season with salt and pepper, to taste, and set aside to cool. Combine ¹/2 cup (125 g/4 oz) whole egg mayonnaise, 2 tablespoons sour cream, 1–2 crushed cloves garlic and lemon juice, to taste, and mix well. Spoon a little of the capsicum mixture onto each blini and top with the mayonnaise mixture and cracked black pepper, to taste.

GOATS CHEESE AND ROASTED CAPSICUM

Cut 3 large red capsicums in half lengthways and remove the seeds. Brush with oil and place, skin-side-up, under a hot grill until the skin blisters and blackens. Cover with a tea towel until cool enough to handle. Remove the skin and cut the flesh into thin strips. Toss in a bowl with 1 crushed clove garlic, a little olive oil, a squeeze of lemon juice, 1 teaspoon soft brown sugar, 2 tablespoons lemon thyme leaves, and salt and pepper to taste. Top the blinis with a capsicum strip and a little crumbled goats cheese.

SALMON AND CREME FRAICHE

Top blinis with a slice of smoked salmon, a small wedge of red onion, a dollop of crème fraîche and a small caperberry.

Blinis, left to right: Bocconcini and Tomato;
Salmon and Crème Fraîche;
Sautéed Vegetable with Garlic Mayonnaise;
Chive Cream and Prosciutto; Roast Beef and
Béarnaise; Goats Cheese and Capsicum

ROAST BEEF AND BEARNAISE

Combine 4 tablespoons white wine vinegar, 2 finely chopped spring onions, 4 whole black peppercorns and a few chopped tarragon sprigs in a small pan. Boil gently until the mixture reduces to about 1 tablespoon. Cool slightly, then strain into a heatproof bowl. Place the bowl over a pan of simmering water, add 2 egg yolks and heat gently, then whisk until smooth. Gradually whisk in 125 g (4 oz) cubed butter, adding one cube at a time. Whisk until the butter is melted and absorbed and the sauce is thickened, then remove from the heat. Top blinis with small pieces of rare roast beef and drizzle with a little of the sauce.

CHIVE CREAM AND PROSCIUTTO

Beat 125 g (4 oz) cream cheese with electric beaters until smooth and creamy. Add 1 tablespoon sour cream, 1 tablespoon whole egg mayonnaise and 2 tablespoons chopped chives and beat until well combined. Spread a little cream cheese mixture onto each blini and top with a little crumbled grilled prosciutto.

41

MUSHROOM PIKELETS WITH CHEESE SAUCE

Preparation time: 25 minutes
+ 30 minutes standing
Total cooking time: 40 minutes
Makes 25–30

Topping
20 g (²/3 oz) butter
100 g (3¹/3 oz) mushrooms,
    chopped
2 tomatoes, peeled and chopped

Cheese Sauce
30 g (1 oz) butter
2 tablespoons plain flour
150 ml (4³/4 fl oz) milk
¹/3 cup (40 g/1¹/3 oz) grated
    Cheddar cheese
2 tablespoons plain yoghurt

1 cup (125 g/4 oz) self-raising
    flour
1 egg, plus 1 egg yolk
300 ml (9²/3 fl oz) milk
25 g (³/4 oz) butter, melted

1 To make Topping: Melt the butter in a frying pan. Add the mushrooms and tomato and cook for 20 minutes, or until pulpy and the liquid has evaporated. Keep warm.

2 To make Cheese Sauce: Melt the butter in a pan. Stir in the flour and cook for 2 minutes. Gradually add the milk, stirring until the mixture boils and thickens. Whisk in the cheese until smooth. Remove from the heat and keep warm.

3 Sift the flour and a pinch of salt into a large bowl and make a well in the centre. Whisk the egg, yolk, milk and melted butter in a jug and pour into the well, whisking until smooth. Cover and set aside for 30 minutes.

4 Heat a lightly greased frying pan. Spoon tablespoonsful of batter into the pan, leaving room for spreading. Cook over medium heat until bubbles appear on the surface and the underside is golden; turn and cook the other side. Remove and cook the remaining batter. Spoon the Topping over the pikelets. Stir the yoghurt into the Cheese Sauce and spoon over the top. Sprinkle with extra cheese and black pepper and place under a hot grill until the cheese is bubbling.

Cook the chopped mushrooms and tomatoes until they have a pulpy consistency.

Stir continuously when adding the milk, until the sauce boils and thickens.

Add the grated cheese to the sauce and whisk until smooth.

Make a well in the centre of the dry ingredients and whisk in the liquid.

TURKEY AND CRANBERRY PIKELETS

Preparation time: 25 minutes
+ 30 minutes standing
Total cooking time: 15 minutes
Makes 25–30

1 cup (125 g/4 oz) self-raising flour
pinch of salt
1 egg, plus 1 egg yolk
300 ml (9²/3 fl oz) milk

25 g (³/4 oz) butter, melted
3 tablespoons mayonnaise
150 g (4³/4 oz) cooked turkey, shredded
3 tablespoons cranberry sauce
1 cup (60 g/2 oz) alfalfa sprouts
3 hard-boiled eggs, sliced

1 Sift the flour and salt into a bowl and make a well in the centre. Whisk the egg, yolk, milk and melted butter in a jug and pour into the well, whisking until just smooth. Cover and set aside for 30 minutes.

2 Heat a frying pan and brush lightly with melted butter or oil. Drop tablespoonsful of the batter into the pan, allowing room for spreading. Cook over medium heat until small bubbles begin to appear on the surface and the underside is golden. Turn the pikelets over and cook the other side. Transfer to a plate, cover with a tea towel and leave to cool while cooking the remaining batter.

3 Spread mayonnaise over each pikelet and top with turkey, cranberry sauce, alfalfa sprouts and egg.

Sift the flour and salt together into a bowl, then make a well in the centre.

Pour the liquid into the well, whisking to make a smooth batter.

Turn the pikelets over when small bubbles appear on the surface.

CHEDDAR BLINIS WITH ROASTED CHERRY TOMATOES AND PESTO

Preparation time: 30 minutes
  + 30 minutes standing
Total cooking time: 25–30 minutes
Serves 6–8

250 g (8 oz) cherry tomatoes
250 g (8 oz) teardrop tomatoes
sea salt and cracked pepper
1 tablespoon lemon thyme sprigs
3 tablespoons pesto

Blinis
7 g (1/4 oz) dried yeast sachet
1 tablespoon caster sugar
1 cup (250 ml/8 fl oz) warm
  milk
3/4 cup (100 g/3 1/3 oz)
  buckwheat flour
3/4 cup (90 g/3 oz) plain flour
1/2 cup (60 g/2 oz) grated
  Cheddar cheese
2 eggs
60 g (2 oz) butter, melted

1 Preheat the oven to moderately hot 200°C (400°F/Gas 6). Place the tomatoes on a non-stick baking tray and sprinkle with sea salt and cracked pepper, to taste. Bake for 20 minutes, or until roasted. Remove from the oven and leave to cool slightly. Fold through the lemon thyme.

2 To make Blinis: Mix together the yeast, sugar and 1/3 cup of the warm milk in a small bowl. Set aside for 10 minutes, or until the mixture is beginning to foam.

3 Sift the flours into a bowl, add the cheese and make a well in the centre. Whisk the eggs, melted butter, yeast mixture and remaining milk in a jug and pour into the well, whisking until the batter is just smooth. Cover and set aside for 30 minutes.

4 Heat a frying pan and brush lightly with melted butter. Add tablespoonsful of batter, allowing room for spreading. Cook over medium heat for about 1 minute, or until the underside is golden. Turn the blinis over and cook the other side. Remove and keep warm while cooking the remaining batter. Place a stack of blinis on each plate and top with pesto and roasted tomatoes.

Bake the tomatoes for 20 minutes, or until they are roasted.

Set the yeast mixture aside for 10 minutes or until it begins to foam.

Make a well in the centre of the dry ingredients and whisk in the liquid.

Use 1 tablespoon of batter for each blini, leaving room for spreading.

Simmer the Marmalade for 30 minutes or until it is thick.

Combine the egg, butter and buttermilk in a small bowl.

Stir the grated beetroot and chopped parsley into the batter.

When the underside is cooked and golden brown, turn the pikelet over.

BEETROOT PIKELETS AND ONION MARMALADE

Preparation time: 25 minutes
Total cooking time: 45 minutes
Serves 4

Onion Marmalade
2 red onions, thinly sliced
2 teaspoons cumin seeds
1 teaspoon black mustard seeds
1/2 cup (125 ml/4 fl oz) balsamic
    vinegar
1/2 cup (95 g/3 1/4 oz) soft brown
    sugar

3/4 cup (90 g/3 oz) plain flour
1/2 teaspoon baking powder
1 egg
30 g (1 oz) butter, melted
1/2 cup (125 ml/4 fl oz)
    buttermilk
1 cup (100 g/3 1/3 oz) grated
    beetroot
1 tablespoon chopped parsley
1/2 cup (125 g/4 oz) plain
    yoghurt, to serve

1 To make Onion Marmalade:
Place the onion, cumin seeds, mustard seeds, vinegar and sugar in a pan and stir over low heat until the sugar has dissolved. Simmer for 30 minutes, or until thick.
2 Sift the flour and baking powder into a bowl and make a well in the centre. Mix together the egg, butter and buttermilk and pour into the well, whisking until just smooth. Stir in the beetroot and chopped fresh parsley.
3 Heat a frying pan and brush lightly with melted butter or oil. Drop tablespoonsful of the batter into the pan, leaving a little room for spreading, and cook over medium heat until the underside is golden.
4 Turn the pikelets over and cook the other side. Remove and cover with a tea towel to keep warm while cooking the remaining batter. Serve topped with yoghurt and Onion Marmalade.

COOK'S FILE

Storage time: Onion Marmalade can be kept for up to 1 week in a jar in the refrigerator. It is also excellent with cold meats and cheeses.
Hint: Wear rubber gloves when grating beetroot as they bleed and can stain your hands.

POTATO ROSTI PIKELETS WITH SOUR CREAM

Preparation time: 20 minutes
Total cooking time: 20 minutes
Makes about 8

3 medium potatoes
(about 500 g/1 lb)
2 tablespoons chopped chives
2 tablespoons grated onion
2 eggs, lightly beaten

¹/₄ cup (30 g/1 oz) self-raising
flour
oil, for shallow-frying
sour cream and chives, to serve

1 Peel and coarsely grate the potatoes, then take small handfuls and squeeze dry. Place in a bowl and add the chives, onion, eggs, sifted flour and salt and pepper to taste. Stir well to combine and moisten.

2 Heat 1 cm (¹/₂ inch) oil in a large frying pan until moderately hot.

3 Drop ¹/₄ cupfuls (60 ml/2 fl oz) of the mixture into the hot oil, cooking two or three pikelets at once. Cook for 3–4 minutes, or until the underside is golden. Turn the pikelets over and cook the other side for 2–3 minutes, or until cooked and golden. Remove and drain on paper towels. Transfer to an ovenproof plate and keep hot in a warm 160°C (315°F/Gas 2–3) oven while cooking the remaining batter. Serve hot with sour cream and a sprinkling of snipped chives.

Squeeze the moisture from the grated potatoes to ensure a crisp finish.

Mix together the ingredients until they are all moistened.

Turn the pikelet over when the underside is cooked and golden brown.

Whisk together the egg, sesame oil, milk and orange juice with a fork.

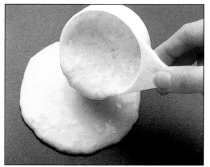

Pour 1/3 cup (80 ml/2³/4 fl oz) batter into the heated frying pan.

Turn the pikelet when bubbles appear on the surface and the underside is golden.

Cut out the shapes using different shaped cookie cutters.

SESAME SHAPES

Preparation time: 35 minutes
Total cooking time: 15–20 minutes
Makes about 15

³/4 cup (90 g/3 oz) self-raising
  flour
2 tablespoons sesame seeds,
  toasted
1 teaspoon grated orange rind
1 egg
1 teaspoon sesame oil
¹/2 cup (125 ml/4 fl oz) milk
2 tablespoons orange juice
60 g (2 oz) sun-dried tomatoes,
  finely chopped

Filling
100 g (3¹/3 oz) soft cream
  cheese
1 tablespoon chopped coriander

1 Sift the flour and a pinch of salt into a bowl, stir in the sesame seeds and grated orange rind and make a well in the centre. With a fork, whisk the egg, sesame oil, milk and orange juice in a jug and pour into the well, whisking until just smooth. Set the batter aside for 15 minutes.
2 Heat a non-stick frying pan and brush lightly with melted butter or oil. Pour ¹/3 cup (80 ml/2³/4 fl oz) batter into the pan and cook over medium heat for 3–4 minutes, or until bubbles appear on the surface and the underside is golden. Turn the pikelet over and cook the other side. Transfer to a plate and cover with a tea towel while cooking the remaining batter.
3 Use cookie cutters to cut out varieties of shapes (you will be sandwiching 3 of each shape together so make sure you have the right number of each).

4 To make Filling: Mix the cream cheese and coriander and use to sandwich together 3 pikelet shapes. Decorate with sun-dried tomato.

GRAVLAX PIKELETS WITH RED CAPSICUM AND TOMATO COULIS

Preparation time: 1 hour
Total cooking time: 25 minutes
Serves 6

Red Capsicum and Tomato Coulis
6 ripe tomatoes
1 large red capsicum
1 small red chilli, seeded and finely chopped (optional)
¼ cup (15 g/½ oz) finely chopped fresh basil

1 cup (125 g/4 oz) self-raising flour
¼ cup (15 g/½ oz) chopped fresh dill
1 egg
20 g (⅔ oz) butter, melted
¾ cup (185 ml/6 fl oz) milk
200 g (6½ oz) gravlax or smoked salmon
1 cup (250 ml/8 fl oz) crème fraîche or sour cream
fresh dill, to garnish

1 To make Red Capsicum and Tomato Coulis: Score a cross in the base of each tomato with a sharp knife. Place the tomatoes in a bowl of boiling water and leave for 2 minutes. Drain and plunge into a bowl of cold water. Peel the skin away from the cross. Cut the tomatoes in half horizontally and scoop out the seeds with a teaspoon. Chop the flesh very finely and place in a bowl.
2 Halve the capsicum and remove the seeds and membrane. Cut into quarters, flatten a little and place, skin-side-up, under a preheated grill for about 10 minutes, or until the skin has blistered and blackened. Place in a paper or plastic bag or cover with a tea towel for 10 minutes (this makes the capsicum sweat, making it easier to remove the skin). Remove the skin from the capsicum, dice the flesh finely and add to the tomatoes. Stir in the chilli, if using, the basil and freshly ground black pepper, to taste.
3 Sift the flour into a bowl, stir in the dill and make a well in the centre. Whisk the egg, melted butter and milk together in a jug and then pour into the well, stirring until the batter is just smooth.
4 Heat a frying pan and brush lightly with melted butter or oil. Spoon heaped tablespoonsful of the batter into the pan, leaving a little room for spreading. Cook the pikelets over medium heat until bubbles appear on the surface.
5 Turn the pikelets over and cook the other side until lightly browned. Transfer to a plate and cover with a tea towel while cooking the remaining batter (the batter should make about 12 pikelets).
6 Place a pikelet into the centre of each plate. Divide the salmon between the pikelets and top with a tablespoon of crème fraîche or sour cream. Top with another pikelet and serve with a generous portion of Red Capsicum and Tomato Coulis and fresh dill.

COOK'S FILE

Note: Gravlax (also spelt Gravadlax) is a Scandinavian delicacy produced by rubbing boned salmon fillets with a salt and sugar mixture and leaving under a heavy weight for 2 days. It is expensive, but well worth the cost.

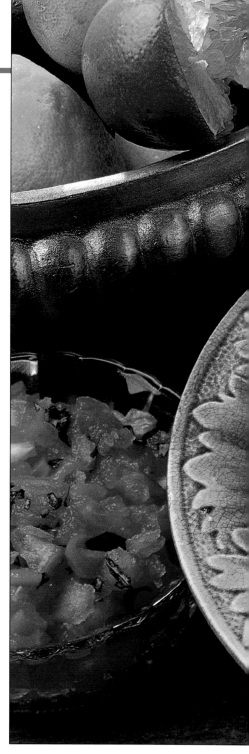

Halve the peeled tomatoes and remove the seeds with a teaspoon.

Grill the capsicum pieces for 10 minutes, or until the skin blackens.

Add the diced capsicum flesh to the chopped tomato.

Sift the flour into a bowl and stir in the chopped fresh dill.

Make a well in the centre of the dry ingredients and stir in the liquid.

Spoon heaped tablespoonsful of the batter into the heated pan.

CRISPY VERMICELLI PIKELETS WITH SESAME VEGETABLES

Preparation time: 15–20 minutes
Total cooking time: 15 minutes
Makes 12

200 g (6½ oz) rice vermicelli
oil, for shallow-frying
1 teaspoon sesame oil
1 carrot, cut into julienne strips
   (see note)
½ red capsicum, cut into
   julienne strips
1 zucchini, cut into julienne
   strips
2 spring onions, cut into
   julienne strips
2 teaspoons oyster sauce

1 Soak the rice vermicelli in boiling water for 3 minutes. Drain thoroughly until the noodles are very dry.
2 Heat the oil in a large heavy-based frying pan over medium heat. Shape tablespoonsful of the noodles into flat discs and shallow-fry for 3 minutes, or until crisp and golden. Drain on paper towels while cooking the remainder.
3 Heat the sesame oil in a non-stick wok and add the julienned vegetables. Stir-fry for 3 minutes, then stir in the oyster sauce and cook for 2 minutes. Serve the vermicelli pikelets topped with the vegetables.

COOK'S FILE

Note: Julienne strips are thin, even-sized pieces of vegetables, about the width of matchsticks. They cook quickly and look very attractive. They can be prepared a couple of hours in advance and stored in an airtight container in the fridge.
Variation: Two-minute noodles can be used instead of vermicelli.

Use a sharp knife to julienne the carrot, capsicum, zucchini and spring onions.

Soak the rice vermicelli in boiling water for about 3 minutes.

Cook the vermicelli discs in hot oil for 3 minutes, or until crisp and golden.

Whisk the lime rind, milk, yoghurt, egg and melted butter with a fork.

Gently stir the chopped smoked salmon into the batter.

Use 2 teaspoons of smoked salmon batter to make each pikelet.

Mix together the sour cream, cumin and lime rind to make the Topping.

SMOKED SALMON PIKELETS WITH LIME CREAM

Preparation time: 25 minutes
+ 20 minutes standing
Total cooking time: 20 minutes
Makes 18–20

3/4 cup (110 g/3²/3 oz)
  wholemeal self-raising flour
1/4 teaspoon bicarbonate of soda
1 teaspoon grated lime rind
1/3 cup (80 ml/2³/4 fl oz) milk
1/3 cup (90 g/3 oz) plain yoghurt
1 egg
30 g (1 oz) butter, melted
100 g (3¹/3 oz) smoked salmon,
  finely chopped
50 g (1²/3 oz) salmon roe
2 tablespoons snipped fresh
  chives

Topping
1/2 cup (125 g/4 oz) sour cream
1 teaspoon ground cumin
1 teaspoon grated lime rind

1 Sift the flour, bicarbonate of soda and a pinch of salt into a bowl and make a well in the centre. Whisk the lime rind, milk, yoghurt, egg and butter in a jug and pour into the well, whisking until the batter is just smooth. Add a little extra milk if the batter is too thick. Stir in the salmon, cover and set aside for 20 minutes.
2 Heat a non-stick frying pan and brush lightly with melted butter or oil. Drop 2 teaspoons batter into the pan to make each pikelet, allowing room for spreading. Cook over low heat for 30 seconds, or until bubbles appear on the surface. Turn over and cook the other side. Remove and cover with a tea towel while cooking the rest.

3 To make Topping: Mix together the sour cream, cumin and lime rind. Spoon over the pikelets and top with salmon roe and snipped fresh chives.

SUN-DRIED TOMATO AND PESTO PIKELETS

Preparation time: 20 minutes
Total cooking time: 15–20 minutes
Makes about 24

2 cups (250 g/8 oz) self-raising
   flour
1/2 teaspoon bicarbonate of soda
1/2 cup (80 g/2²/3 oz) finely
   chopped sun-dried tomatoes
1 tablespoon finely chopped
   fresh basil
1 tablespoon finely chopped
   pine nuts

1 clove garlic, crushed
1/4 cup (25 g/3/4 oz) freshly
   grated Parmesan
2 eggs
1¹/3 cups (350 ml/11 fl oz) milk
fresh mascarpone and char-
   grilled capsicum, to serve

1 Sift the flour and bicarbonate of soda into a bowl. Add the sun-dried tomato, basil, pine nuts, garlic and Parmesan; mix to combine and make a well in the centre.
2 Whisk the eggs and milk in a jug and pour into the well, stirring until just smooth. Season to taste with salt and pepper.

3 Heat a non-stick frying pan and brush lightly with melted butter or oil. Drop heaped tablespoonsful of batter into the pan, allowing room for spreading. Cook the pikelets over medium heat until bubbles appear on the surface and the underside is golden. Turn over and cook the other side. Transfer to a plate and cover with a tea towel to keep warm while cooking the remaining batter. Serve in a stack with fresh mascarpone and strips of char-grilled capsicum.

COOK'S FILE

Note: If you use sun-dried tomatoes in oil, drain them thoroughly.

Add the sun-dried tomato, basil, pinenuts, garlic and Parmesan.

Make a well in the centre of the dry ingredients and stir in the liquid.

Brush a non-stick frying pan with a little melted butter or oil.

PRAWN PIKELETS WITH CHILLI SAUCE

Preparation time: 20 minutes
   + 30 minutes standing
Total cooking time: 25 minutes
Makes 28

1 cup (125 g/4 oz) self-raising
   flour
1 egg, plus 1 egg yolk
300 ml (9²/3 fl oz) milk

25 g (3/4 oz) butter, melted
2 tablespoons chopped fresh
   coriander
14 cooked prawns, peeled
sweet chilli sauce, to serve

1 Sift the flour and a pinch of salt into a bowl and make a well in the centre. With a fork, whisk the egg, yolk, milk and butter in a jug and pour into the well, stirring until the batter is just smooth. Cover and set aside for 30 minutes.

2 Stir the coriander into the batter. Cut the prawns in half lengthways. Heat a frying pan and brush with melted butter or oil.
3 Drop tablespoonsful of batter into the pan, leaving room for spreading, and place a prawn half on top of each one. Cook over medium heat until bubbles appear on the surface and the underside is golden. Turn over and cook the other side. Remove and keep warm. Cook the remaining batter. Drizzle with chilli sauce to serve.

Whisk together the whole egg, egg yolk, milk and butter with a fork.

Leave the batter to stand for 30 minutes, then stir in the chopped coriander.

Place a prawn half, cut-side-down, in the centre of each pikelet.

Sun-dried Tomato and Pesto Pikelets (Top), and Prawn Pikelets with Chilli Sauce

SPINACH, FETA AND OLIVE PIKELETS WITH FRESH TOMATO SALSA

Preparation time: 35 minutes
  + 1 hour standing
Total cooking time: 15–20 minutes
Makes 25

Fresh Tomato Salsa
1 small red chilli, seeded and
  chopped
3 large ripe tomatoes, peeled,
  seeded and chopped
2 spring onions, finely sliced
1 small red onion, finely
  chopped

1 tablespoon chopped fresh
  coriander
1/2 teaspoon cracked pepper
1 tablespoon light olive oil
1 tablespoon lime juice

1 cup (45 g/1 1/2 oz) firmly
  packed baby English spinach
  leaves
2 cups (250 g/8 oz) self-raising
  flour
2 tablespoons caster sugar
1/3 cup (40 g/1 1/3 oz) sliced
  black olives
2 eggs, lightly beaten
1 1/2 cups (375 ml/12 fl oz) milk
90 g (3 oz) feta cheese,
  crumbled

1 To make Fresh Tomato Salsa: Combine all the ingredients in a bowl, cover and set aside for at least 1 hour.
2 Wash, dry and finely shred the spinach. Sift the flour into a bowl, add the sugar, spinach and olives and mix well. Add the eggs and milk and stir until just smooth. Stir in the feta and season with pepper, to taste.
3 Heat a frying pan and brush lightly with melted butter or oil. Add heaped tablespoonsful of batter, allowing room for spreading. Cook over medium heat until bubbles form on the surface and the underside is golden. Turn over and cook. Remove and keep warm. Cook the remaining batter. Serve with Tomato Salsa.

Wear gloves to prevent burning when you finely chop the chilli.

Using a sharp knife, shred the washed and dried baby spinach.

Stir the crumbled feta cheese into the batter and season to taste with pepper.

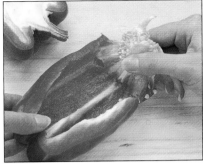

Remove the seeds and membrane from the capsicum.

Removed the blackened skin from the grilled capsicum.

Add the buttermilk mixture all at once to the well in the dry ingredients.

Stir the capsicum, corn kernels and chives through the batter.

CAPSICUM PIKELETS WITH PROSCIUTTO

Preparation time: 30 minutes
  + 10 minutes resting
Total cooking time: 25 minutes
Makes about 20

1 small red capsicum
1 cup (125 g/4 oz) plain flour
1/2 teaspoon bicarbonate of soda
1 1/4 cups (315 ml/10 fl oz)
    buttermilk
1 egg
50 g (1 2/3 oz) butter, melted
130 g (4 1/4 oz) can corn kernels,
    drained
1 tablespoon finely chopped
    chives
1 cup (250 ml/8 fl oz) crème
    fraîche
5 slices prosciutto, cut into
    strips
snipped chives, to serve

1 Remove the seeds and membrane from the capsicum. Cut into large flat pieces and place, skin-side-up, under a hot grill. Cook for 10 minutes, or until blackened. Place in a paper or plastic bag for 10 minutes, then peel away the skin. Chop the flesh finely.

2 Sift the flour, bicarbonate of soda and a pinch of salt into a bowl and make a well in the centre. Whisk the buttermilk, egg and melted butter in a jug and pour into the well all at once. Stir until just moistened and then stir through the capsicum, corn and chives. Do not overmix.

3 Heat a frying pan and brush with melted butter or oil. Drop 2 teaspoonsful of batter into the pan for each pikelet, leaving a little room for spreading. Cook until bubbles begin to form on the surface and the underside is golden brown.

4 Turn the pikelets over and cook the other side. Transfer to a plate and cover with a tea towel to keep warm while cooking the remaining batter. Top each pikelet with a teaspoon of crème fraîche and some strips of prosciutto and garnish with chives.

55

CREPES

CREPES WITH SUGAR, LEMON AND CREAM

Preparation time: 20 minutes
+ 30 minutes standing
Total cooking time: 20–25 minutes
Makes about 14 crepes

1 cup (125 g/4 oz) plain flour
1 egg
300 ml (9²/₃ fl oz) milk
30 g (1 oz) butter
sugar, lemons and clotted cream

1 Sift the flour and a pinch of salt into a large bowl and make a well in the centre. Gradually whisk in the combined egg and milk until the batter is smooth and free of lumps. Cover and set aside for 30 minutes.

2 Transfer the batter to a jug for easier pouring. Heat a small crepe or non-stick frying pan. Place the butter on 2–3 sheets of paper towels and scrunch up to make a bundle. Use this to lightly grease the pan (this helps ensure it is not overgreased).

3 Pour some batter into the pan, swirling to thinly cover the base, and pour off any excess. If necessary, add 2–3 teaspoons milk to thin the batter. Cook for about 20 seconds, or until the edges just begin to curl, then turn over and lightly brown the other side. Transfer to a plate and keep warm while cooking the remaining batter, greasing the pan whenever necessary.

4 Sprinkle the crepes with sugar and a little lemon juice and fold into quarters. Place 2 or 3 on each plate and top with a dollop of clotted cream.

Sift the flour and salt into a bowl large enough to hold all the batter.

Pour the egg mixture into the well in the dry ingredients and whisk until smooth.

Put the butter in paper towels and scrunch into a bundle to grease the pan.

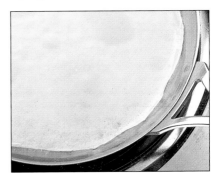

Cook the crepe for about 20 seconds, or until the edges just begin to curl.

BANANA CREPES WITH BUTTERSCOTCH SAUCE

Preparation time: 30 minutes
+ 30 minutes standing
Total cooking time: 45 minutes
Makes about 16 crepes

1 cup (125 g/4 oz) plain flour
1 egg, plus 1 egg yolk
1¹/2 cups (375 ml/12 fl oz)
    buttermilk
60 g (2 oz) butter
¹/2 cup (115 g/3³/4 oz) firmly
    packed soft brown sugar
¹/2 cup (125 ml/4 fl oz)
    sweetened condensed milk
2 tablespoons golden syrup
1 cup (250 ml/8 fl oz) hot milk
¹/2 cup (75 g/2¹/2 oz) currants
1 tablespoon rum or brandy
¹/2 cup (70 g/2¹/3 oz) hazelnuts
4 bananas

1 Mix the flour, egg, egg yolk and half the buttermilk in a food processor for 10 seconds. Add the remaining buttermilk and 30 g (1 oz) melted butter and process until smooth. Pour into a jug, cover and set aside for 30 minutes. Heat a small crepe pan and brush lightly with melted butter. Pour ¹/4 cup (60 ml/2 fl oz) batter into the pan, swirling quickly to thinly cover the base. Cook for 30 seconds, then turn and cook the other side until lightly browned. Set aside, covered, while cooking the remaining batter.
2 Place the brown sugar, condensed milk, golden syrup and remaining butter in a small pan and stir over low heat until the sugar dissolves. Simmer for 2 minutes and remove from the heat. Beat in the hot milk a teaspoonful at a time (if it is added too quickly the mixture will curdle). Return to the heat and simmer for 1 minute. Cover and set aside.
3 Combine the currants with the rum or brandy. Toast the hazelnuts under a hot grill, then rub with a clean cloth to remove the skins; roughly chop.
4 Preheat the oven to warm 160°C (315°F/Gas 2–3). Thinly slice the bananas and arrange over a quarter of each crepe. Scatter with soaked currants and drizzle with a little sauce. Fold the crepes into quarters, then arrange in fours on ovenproof plates. Cover with foil and place in the oven for 10–15 minutes, or until hot. Drizzle with more sauce and scatter with hazelnuts.

Swirl the pan quickly to spread the batter evenly and thinly over the base.

Beat the hot milk into the sauce mixture, a teaspoonful at a time.

Rub the toasted hazelnuts with a clean tea towel to remove the skins.

CREME FRAICHE CREPE STACK WITH TAMARILLO

Preparation time: 40 minutes
Total cooking time: 30 minutes
Serves 6

1 cup (130 g/4¼ oz) buckwheat
    flour
pinch of salt
2 tablespoons soft brown sugar
3 eggs
30 g (1 oz) butter, melted
1 cup (250 ml/8 fl oz) milk
1 tablespoon brandy
6 tamarillos
½ cup (125 g/4 oz) sugar
2 cups (500 ml/16 fl oz) water
1 cinnamon stick

Crème Fraîche Filling
200 g (6½ oz) crème fraîche or
    light sour cream
½ teaspoon ground cinnamon
2 tablespoons soft brown sugar
200 g (6½ oz) hazelnuts,
    roasted and roughly chopped

1 Sift the flour, salt and sugar into a bowl and make a well in the centre. Mix the eggs, butter, milk and brandy in a small jug and gradually whisk into the well to form a smooth batter. Heat a small crepe or non-stick frying pan and brush lightly with melted butter. Pour ¼ cup (60 ml/2 fl oz) batter into the pan, swirling quickly to thinly cover the base. Cook over moderate heat for 1 minute, or until the underside is golden. Turn and cook the other side until golden. Remove, cover and keep warm while cooking the remaining batter.
2 Place the tamarillos in a large pan of boiling water for 3 minutes, then remove. Cool slightly, then peel off the skins and discard. Place the sugar and water in a pan; stir over low heat until the sugar dissolves. Add the tamarillos and cinnamon and simmer for 5 minutes. Remove the tamarillos, cover and keep warm. Bring the syrup to the boil and then simmer for 15 minutes, or until reduced by half. Discard the cinnamon stick.

3 **To make Crème Fraîche Filling:** Mix together all the ingredients. Spread each crepe evenly with some filling, then carefully stack. Cut the stack into wedges; serve with a tamarillo, syrup and thick cream.

COOK'S FILE

Variation: Use poached oranges or quinces instead of tamarillos.

Gradually add the milk mixture to the dry ingredients, whisking to form a batter.

When one side of the crepe is golden, turn it over and cook the other side.

Carefully peel the skins from the lightly poached tamarillos.

CREPES WITH ORANGE AND ALMOND BUTTER

Preparation time: 30 minutes
  + 30 minutes standing
Total cooking time: 30 minutes
Makes 12 crepes

3/4 cup (90 g/3 oz) plain flour
1 egg, plus 1 egg yolk
1 cup (250 ml/8 fl oz) milk
30 g (1 oz) butter, melted
1 tablespoon Grand Marnier or
    Cointreau (optional)
icing sugar, to serve

Orange and Almond Butter
100 g (3¹/3 oz) butter
2 tablespoons caster sugar
¹/2 cup (95 g/3¹/4 oz) ground
    almonds
few drops of almond essence
1 tablespoon grated orange rind
2 tablespoons orange juice
2 tablespoons Grand Marnier or
    Cointreau

1 Mix the flour, egg, egg yolk and half the milk in a food processor for 10 seconds. Add the remaining milk, butter and liqueur, if using, and process until smooth. Pour into a jug, cover and set aside for 30 minutes.

2 Heat a medium crepe or non-stick frying pan and brush lightly with melted butter. Pour ¹/4 cup (60 ml/ 2 fl oz) batter into the pan, swirling to cover the base thinly (add a little milk if the batter is too thick). Cook for about 30 seconds. Turn over and cook the other side for 20 seconds. Transfer to a plate and cover with a tea towel while cooking the remaining batter. (The crepes can be kept for several hours and filled just before baking.)

3 **To make Orange and Almond Butter:** Beat the butter with electric beaters until creamy. Gradually add the sugar and ground almonds. Beat in the essence, rind, juice and liqueur.

4 Preheat the oven to moderate 180ºC (350ºF/Gas 4). Spread each crepe with a tablespoon of Orange and Almond Butter and fold in half, then into quarters. Put the crepes, overlapping, in a greased ovenproof dish and sprinkle with icing sugar. Bake for 10–15 minutes, or until heated through. Serve with ice cream.

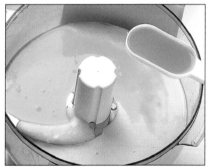

Add the remaining milk, melted butter and liqueur to the batter mixture.

Cook the crepe for 30 seconds, then turn over with a spatula.

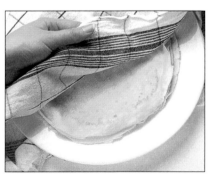

Transfer the crepes to a plate and cover with a tea towel to keep warm.

Beat the essence, rind, juice and liqueur into the Almond Butter.

FRUIT COMPOTE WITH CRISPY CREPE BOWS

Preparation time: 30 minutes
Total cooking time: 45 minutes
Serves 6

Dried Fruit Compote
375 g (12 oz) dried fruit salad
125 g (4 oz) dried figs,
    quartered
1/2 cup (60 g/2 oz) raisins
1 1/4 cups (315 ml/10 fl oz)
    sweet dessert wine
1 bay leaf
1 cinnamon stick
1 star anise

1 cup (175 g/5 2/3 oz) rice flour
2 tablespoons caster sugar
1 egg
1 teaspoon vanilla essence
1 tablespoon grated orange rind
1 1/2 cups (375 ml/12 fl oz) milk
oil, for deep-frying
icing sugar, to dust

1 To make Dried Fruit Compote:
Place all the compote ingredients in a
pan. Bring to the boil, reduce the heat
and simmer for 15 minutes, or until the
fruit is plump and tender. Remove and
discard the spices and the bay leaf.
2 Sift the flour and sugar into a bowl
and make a well in the centre. Whisk
together the egg, vanilla essence, rind
and milk and gradually pour into the
well, whisking until just smooth. Heat
a small crepe or non-stick frying pan
and brush lightly with melted butter.
Pour 1/4 cup (60 ml/2 fl oz) batter into
the pan, swirling quickly to thinly
coat the base. Cook over moderate
heat for 1 minute, or until the
underside is golden. Turn over and

cook for 1 minute. Remove and cover
while cooking the remaining batter.
3 Using a pastry wheel, cut each
crepe into 2 cm (3/4 inch) wide strips.
Gently tie each strip into a knot.
Deep-fry the strips in batches in
moderately hot oil until crisp and
golden. Remove with a slotted spoon;

drain on paper towels. Dust with icing
sugar and serve with the compote.

COOK'S FILE

Variation: Any dried fruit can be
used instead of mixed fruit salad. The
compote can be prepared in advance—
keep, covered, in the refrigerator.

*Use tongs to remove the cinnamon stick,
star anise and bay leaf.*

*Make a well in the centre of the dry
ingredients and whisk in the liquid.*

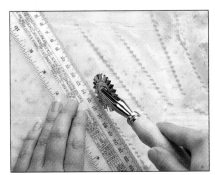

*Using a pastry wheel, cut the crepes into
strips about 2 cm (3/4 inch) wide.*

SHREDDED COCONUT CREPES WITH PALM SUGAR SYRUP

Preparation time: 40 minutes
+ 1 hour standing
Total cooking time: 45 minutes
Makes about 12 crepes

Shredded Coconut Filling
185 g (6 oz) palm sugar, roughly
    chopped
1½ cups (375 ml/12 fl oz)
    water
2 cups (120 g/4 oz) shredded
    coconut
½ cup (125 ml/4 fl oz) coconut
    cream

1 cup (125 g/4 oz) plain flour
1 egg
1 cup (250 ml/8 fl oz) coconut
    cream
½ cup (125 ml/4 fl oz) water
mango or pineapple slices, to
    serve

1 To make Shredded Coconut Filling: Place the sugar and water in a small heavy-based pan. Stir over low heat until the sugar is dissolved, then simmer for 15 minutes to make a syrup. Place the coconut in a bowl with ⅔ cup (170 ml/5½ fl oz) of the syrup and the coconut cream and stir to combine. Return the pan with the remaining palm sugar syrup to the heat and simmer for 15 minutes, or until reduced to a thick, sticky syrup.

2 Mix the flour, egg, coconut cream and water in a food processor for 10 seconds, or until smooth. Transfer to a jug for easier pouring, cover and set aside for 1 hour.

3 Heat a small crepe pan and brush lightly with melted butter. Pour just enough batter into the pan, swirling, to cover the base; pour off the excess. Cook for about 30 seconds, then turn over and cook the other side. Remove and cover with a tea towel while cooking the remaining batter.

4 Place 1 tablespoon of Shredded Coconut Filling in the centre of each crepe. Roll each crepe up firmly, folding in the edges to form a parcel. Serve with sliced fresh mango or pineapple and drizzle with the remaining palm sugar syrup.

Add the coconut cream and palm sugar syrup to the coconut and stir to combine.

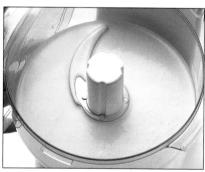

Process the flour, egg, coconut cream and water for 10 seconds, or until smooth.

Swirl the pan to coat the base thinly with the batter.

Roll the filled crepes up firmly, taking care to fold in the edges.

HAZELNUT PRALINE CREPES WITH CHOCOLATE SAUCE

Preparation time: 1 hour
  + 30 minutes standing
Total cooking time: 45 minutes
Makes about 10 crepes

100 g (3¹/₃ oz) hazelnuts
¹/₃ cup (90 g/3 oz) caster sugar,
    plus 2 tablespoons
90 g (3 oz) unsalted butter, at
    room temperature
1 cup (125 g/4 oz) plain flour
1 egg, plus 1 egg yolk
1¹/₄ cups (315 ml/10 fl oz) milk
50 g (1²/₃ oz) butter
125 g (4 oz) dark chocolate,
    chopped
2 tablespoons sifted icing sugar
¹/₂ cup (125 g/4 oz) sour cream
2 tablespoons Kahlua or
    Tia Maria

1 Toast the hazelnuts under a low grill then rub off the skins with a tea towel. Roughly chop a third of the nuts and set aside. Put the remaining nuts on an oiled oven tray. Put ¹/₃ cup (90 g/3 oz) sugar with 2 tablespoons water in a pan. Stir over low heat, without boiling, until the sugar has dissolved. Simmer, without stirring, for 5 minutes, or until golden brown. Quickly pour over the whole nuts and allow to set. Finely chop in a food processor to form praline.
2 Beat the unsalted butter and remaining sugar with electric beaters until creamy. Stir in two-thirds of the praline, cover and keep cool.
3 Mix the flour, egg, egg yolk and half the milk in a food processor for 10 seconds. Add the remaining milk

and 20 g (²/₃ oz) melted butter and process until smooth. Pour into a jug, cover and set aside for 30 minutes. Heat a medium crepe pan and brush with melted butter. Pour ¹/₄ cup (60 ml/2 fl oz) batter into the pan, swirling to cover the base. Cook for 30 seconds; turn and cook the other side. Remove and repeat with the remaining batter.
4 Heat the chocolate and remaining butter in a heatproof bowl over a pan of simmering water. Once melted, add the icing sugar, sour cream and liqueur. Stir until smooth and glossy.

5 Preheat the oven to warm 160°C (315°F/Gas 2–3). Spread each crepe with a tablespoon of the praline butter. Roll up into cigar shapes and place in a greased ovenproof dish in a single layer. Bake for 10 minutes, or until warm. Sprinkle with the chopped hazelnuts and remaining praline. Serve with warm chocolate sauce and ice cream.

COOK'S FILE

Note: Praline may be made in advance and stored in an airtight jar in the refrigerator.

Quickly pour the golden toffee over the whole nuts on the tray.

Brush the heated pan with melted butter and then pour in the batter.

Add the icing sugar, sour cream and liqueur to the melted chocolate mixture.

ORANGE LIQUEUR CREPES

Preparation time: 30 minutes +
30 minutes resting
Total cooking time: 30–40 minutes
Makes 12–14 crepes

1 cup (125 g/4 oz) plain flour
1 tablespoon sugar
1/2 cup (125 ml/4 fl oz) milk
1/2 cup (125 ml/4 fl oz) water
2 egg yolks
1/4 cup (60 ml/2 fl oz) rum or
brandy
60 g (2 oz) butter, melted

Orange Butter
200 g (6¹/2 oz) softened butter
2 tablespoons finely grated
orange rind
1/3 cup (90 g/3 oz) sugar
2 tablespoons icing sugar
1/2 cup (125 ml/4 fl oz) orange
juice
1/4 cup (60 ml/2 fl oz) Grand
Marnier

1 Process the flour, sugar, milk, water, egg yolks, rum or brandy and butter in a food processor or blender until the batter is smooth and free of lumps. Pour into a jug, cover and set aside for at least 30 minutes.
2 To make Orange Butter: Process the butter in a food processor until creamy. Add the rind, sugar and icing sugar and process to combine. With the motor running, add 1/2 teaspoon at a time of the combined orange juice and Grand Marnier, blending well after each addition.
3 Heat a small crepe pan and lightly grease with melted butter. Pour in just enough batter, swirling, to thinly cover the base of the pan. Cook for about 20 seconds, or until the edges just begin to curl. Turn over and lightly brown the other side. Remove and cook the rest of the crepes, greasing the pan when necessary.
4 Place the Orange Butter in a large frying pan and heat until foaming. Working quickly using tongs, with one crepe at a time, dip both sides of the crepe into the pan, then fold into quarters. Serve with ice cream.

COOK'S FILE

Note: For traditional Crêpes Suzette, dip each crepe in the Orange Butter and fold in the pan, then push to one side, continuing until all crepes are folded in the pan. Pour over a little liqueur and flambé with a match.

Place all the ingredients for the batter in a food processor.

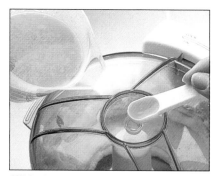

With the motor running, gradually add 1/2 teaspoonsful of the juice mixture.

Use tongs to dip the crepes in the butter and then fold into quarters.

Swirl the pan quickly to thinly coat the base with the batter.

Beat together the ricotta, egg yolks, caster sugar, lemon rind and juice.

Place a heaped tablespoon of Ricotta Filling onto each crepe, then fold up.

Place the filled crepes in an ovenproof dish and brush lightly with melted butter.

RICOTTA BLINTZES

Preparation time: 30 minutes
  + 1 hour standing
Total cooking time: 30–40 minutes
Makes about 14

1 cup (125 g/4 oz) plain flour
2 eggs
1¼ cups (315 ml/10 fl oz) milk
30 g (1 oz) butter, melted

Ricotta Filling
½ cup (60 g/2 oz) raisins
1 tablespoon Grand Marnier or
  Cointreau
375 g (12 oz) fresh ricotta
2 egg yolks
⅓ cup (90 g/3 oz) caster sugar
1 tablespoon grated lemon rind
2 tablespoons lemon juice
20 g (⅔ oz) butter, melted
icing sugar, to dust

1 Place the flour, eggs and half the milk in a food processor and mix for 10 seconds. Add the remaining milk and butter and process until smooth. Pour the mixture into a jug; cover and set aside for 30 minutes.

2 Heat a medium crepe pan; brush with melted butter. Pour enough batter into the pan, swirling quickly, to thinly cover the base (add a little milk if the batter is too thick). Pour back any excess. Cook for 30 seconds, turn and cook the other side. Remove and cook the remaining batter.

3 To make Ricotta Filling: Put the raisins in a bowl and mix with the liqueur; set aside for 30 minutes. Beat the ricotta, yolks, caster sugar, rind and juice for 1–2 minutes, or until smooth. Stir in the raisins and liqueur.

4 Preheat the oven to warm 160°C (315°F/Gas 2–3). Place a heaped tablespoon of filling on the centre of each crepe, then fold into a flat parcel. Place the filled crepes, fold-side-down, in a greased ovenproof dish in a single layer. Brush each crepe lightly with the melted butter. Cover with foil and bake for 10–15 minutes, or until hot. Serve with a light dusting of sifted icing sugar.

COOK'S FILE

Hint: Ricotta Blintzes may be assembled several hours in advance and heated just prior to serving.

AMARETTI APPLE STACK WITH CARAMEL SAUCE

Preparation time: 40 minutes
  + 30 minutes standing
Total cooking time: 1 hour
Serves 4–6

1 cup (125 g/4 oz) plain flour
2 eggs
1 cup (250 ml/8 fl oz) milk
1½ tablespoons melted butter
1 tablespoon amaretti, optional
125 g (4 oz) amaretti biscuits
5 green apples, peeled and
  cored
185 g (6 oz) butter
1 cup (185 g/6 oz) soft brown
  sugar
½ cup (175 g/5⅔ oz) golden
  syrup
½ cup (125 ml/4 fl oz) cream
¾ cup (185 g/6 oz) light sour
  cream

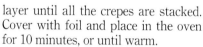

1 Mix the flour, eggs and half the milk in a food processor for 10 seconds. Add the remaining milk, the melted butter and amaretti and process until smooth. Pour into a jug, cover and leave for 30 minutes. Heat a small crepe pan and brush with melted butter. Pour batter into the pan, swirling quickly, to thinly cover the base. Cook for 30 seconds, turn, and cook the other side until lightly browned. Remove; repeat with the remaining batter to make 10 crepes.
2 Preheat the oven to moderate 180°C (350°F/Gas 4). Roughly chop the biscuits in a food processor. Place on an oven tray and bake for 5–8 minutes, stirring occasionally, until crisp. Cut the apples into very thin slices and mix in a bowl with 60 g (2 oz) of the butter,

melted, and half the brown sugar. Spread evenly onto a tray and place under a moderate grill for 5 minutes. Turn and grill until light brown and soft (you may need to do this in batches). Set aside.
3 Put a crepe on a large heatproof serving plate. Spread evenly with some apple, slightly mounded in the middle, and sprinkle with chopped amaretti biscuits. Continue to fill and

layer until all the crepes are stacked. Cover with foil and place in the oven for 10 minutes, or until warm.
4 Put the remaining brown sugar with the syrup, cream and remaining butter in a small pan. Stir over low heat until the sugar dissolves, then simmer for 1 minute. Spread the top crepe with sour cream. Pour a little warm sauce over the stack and cut into wedges to serve.

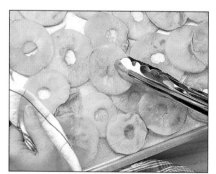

Grill the apple slices for 5 minutes, then turn over and grill the other side.

Spread each crepe with apple and sprinkle with the chopped amaretti biscuits.

Combine the brown sugar, golden syrup, cream and butter in a small pan.

STRAWBERRY RICOTTA CREPES WITH ORANGE LIQUEUR SAUCE

Preparation time: 40 minutes
  + 30 minutes standing
Total cooking time: 30 minutes
Makes about 12 crepes

3/4 cup (90 g/3 oz) plain flour
1 egg, plus 1 egg yolk
3/4 cup (185 ml/6 fl oz) milk
20 g (2/3 oz) butter, melted
fresh berries, to serve

Ricotta Cream Filling
350 g (11 1/4 oz) fresh ricotta
1/4 cup (60 ml/2 fl oz) cream
1 tablespoon caster sugar
1 teaspoon vanilla essence
300 g (9 2/3 oz) strawberries,
    hulled and sliced

Orange Liqueur Sauce
1/2 teaspoon grated orange rind
3/4 cup (185 ml/6 fl oz) fresh
    orange juice
2 tablespoons caster sugar
2 tablespoons Grand Marnier or
    Cointreau
1 tablespoon cornflour
30 g (1 oz) butter

1 Mix the flour, egg, egg yolk and half the milk in a food processor for 10 seconds. Add the butter and remaining milk and process until smooth. Transfer to a jug for easier pouring, cover and set the batter aside for 30 minutes.

2 To make Ricotta Cream Filling: Beat together the ricotta, cream, sugar and vanilla essence until smooth. Fold in the strawberries, cover and refrigerate.

3 To make Orange Liqueur Sauce: Place the orange rind, juice, sugar and liqueur in a small pan. Blend the cornflour and 3 tablespoons water until smooth; add to the pan. Stir over low heat for 3–4 minutes, or until the mixture boils and thickens; add the butter and stir for 1 minute more. Cover and set aside.

4 Heat a small crepe pan and brush lightly with melted butter. Pour enough batter into the pan, swirling, to thinly coat the base; pour the excess back into the jug. If the batter is too thick add a little more milk. Cook for 30 seconds, turn and cook the other side until lightly browned. Remove and cook the rest.

5 Place a crepe on a serving plate and spread evenly with filling. Fold the crepe in half, then in half again diagonally. Pour the sauce over the top and scatter with berries. Repeat with the remaining crepes.

Use a metal spoon to gently fold the strawberries into the ricotta filling.

Stir the Orange Sauce over low heat until the mixture boils and thickens.

Spread the Ricotta Cream Filling evenly over the crepes.

ALMOND MASCARPONE CREPES WITH SUMMER FRUIT

Preparation time: 40 minutes
+ 30 minutes standing
Total cooking time: 35 minutes
Makes about 12 crepes

Almond Mascarpone
60 g (2 oz) slivered almonds
1/2 cup (125 g/4 oz) caster sugar
500 g (1 lb) mascarpone

250 g (8 oz) fresh strawberries,
    hulled and sliced
1 tablespoon Grand Marnier or
    Cointreau
1 tablespoon caster sugar
1 cup (125 g/4 oz) plain flour
2 eggs
1/2 cup (125 ml/4 fl oz) milk
30 g (1 oz) butter, melted
4 kiwi fruit, thinly sliced
200 g (6 1/2 oz) fresh raspberries
250 g (8 oz) fresh blueberries

1 To make Almond Mascarpone:
Toast the almonds under a low grill
until lightly golden; place on an oiled
oven tray. Put the caster sugar in a
small heavy-based pan with 1/2 cup
(125 ml/4 fl oz) water and stir, without
boiling, until the sugar has dissolved.
Bring to the boil, then reduce the heat
and simmer, without stirring, for
15 minutes, or until the liquid turns
golden brown. Quickly pour over the
almonds and leave to set. Finely grind
in a food processor and transfer to a
bowl. Stir in the mascarpone, cover
and refrigerate.
2 Place the strawberries in a large
bowl and sprinkle with the liqueur
and caster sugar. Refrigerate.

3 Mix the flour, eggs and milk in a
food processor for 10 seconds. Add
1/2 cup (125 ml/4 fl oz) water and the
butter and process until smooth. Pour
into a jug; set aside for 30 minutes.
Heat a small crepe pan or non-stick
frying pan and brush lightly with
melted butter. Pour 1/4 cup (60 ml/
2 fl oz) batter into the pan, swirling to
cover the base thinly. Cook for about
30 seconds; turn the crepe over and
cook the other side until lightly
browned. Remove to a plate and cover
while cooking the remaining batter.
Spread each crepe with Almond
Mascarpone and fold into quarters.
Serve with macerated strawberries
and the other fruit.

*Stir the water and sugar together,
without boiling, until the sugar dissolves.*

*When the almond mixture is set, finely
grind in a food processor.*

*Add the water and melted butter to the
combined flour, eggs and milk.*

Simmer until the figs are plump and the liquid has reduced.

Mix together the mascarpone, brown sugar and cream.

Make a well in the centre of the dry ingredients and whisk in the liquid.

Use a spatula to turn the crepe over and cook the other side.

COCONUT CREPES WITH LIQUEUR FIGS

Preparation time: 30 minutes
Total cooking time: 30 minutes
Serves 4

Liqueur Figs
375 g (12 oz) dried figs
1 tablespoon soft brown sugar
1 cup (250 ml/8 fl oz) orange
    juice
¼ cup (60 ml/2 fl oz) brandy
1 bay leaf
3 cloves
1 cinnamon stick

Mascarpone Cream
150 g (4³/4 oz) mascarpone
2 tablespoons soft brown sugar
2 tablespoons thick cream

½ cup (60 g/2 oz) plain flour
2 eggs
1 teaspoon coconut liqueur
2 teaspoons oil
³/4 cup (185 ml/6 fl oz) milk
1 cup (60 g/2 oz) shredded
    coconut, toasted

1 To make Liqueur Figs: Place the figs, sugar, orange juice, brandy, bay leaf, cloves and cinnamon stick in a pan. Simmer for 20 minutes, or until the figs are plump and the liquid has reduced by two-thirds.

2 To make Mascarpone Cream: Gently mix together the mascarpone, sugar and cream.

3 Sift the flour and a pinch of salt into a bowl and make a well in the centre. Whisk the eggs, liqueur, oil and milk in a jug, then gradually pour into the well, whisking until just smooth. Fold in the coconut.

4 Heat a crepe pan and brush lightly with melted butter or oil. Add ¼ cup (60 ml/2 fl oz) batter to the pan and spread with the back of a spoon. Cook over moderate heat for 1 minute, or until the underside is golden; turn over and cook the other side. Transfer to a plate and cover with a tea towel while cooking the remaining batter.

5 Place a few drained figs in the centre of each crepe. Fold the crepes up and around the figs to form bags and tie with string. Dust lightly with icing sugar and serve with Mascarpone Cream.

COOK'S FILE

Note: Mascarpone is a soft cream cheese from Lombardy, Italy, sold in a plastic tub at most delicatessens.

SUSHI CREPES

Preparation time: 1 hour
Total cooking time: about 30 minutes
Makes about 40

Egg Crepes
4 eggs
2 tablespoons cold water
pinch of salt

Sushi
1 cup (220 g/7 oz) short-grain
    rice
2 cups (500 ml/16 fl oz) water
2 tablespoons rice vinegar
1 tablespoon sugar
1 teaspoon salt
1 tablespoon mirin or dry sherry
a little wasabi
125 g (4 oz) sashimi tuna, cut
    into thin strips
1 small cucumber, peeled and
    cut into matchsticks
1/2 avocado, peeled and cut into
    matchsticks
3 tablespoons pickled ginger,
    cut into thin strips
soy sauce, for dipping

1 To make Egg Crepes: Place the eggs, water and salt in a bowl and whisk gently to combine. Heat and lightly oil a small crepe pan, and pour enough of the egg mixture into the pan to lightly cover the base. Cook over low heat for 1 minute; do not allow the egg crepes to brown. Turn the crepe over and cook the other side for 1 minute. Transfer to a plate and cook the remaining batter.

2 To make Sushi: Place the rice and water in a pan, bring to boil, then reduce the heat and simmer for 5 minutes, or until small tunnels begin to appear in the rice. If using gas, cover and turn the heat to very low, and continue cooking for 7 minutes, or until all the liquid is absorbed. If using an electric stovetop, remove the pan from the heat, cover and leave the rice to steam for 10–12 minutes (this prevents the rice from catching on the bottom of the pan and burning).

3 Combine the rice vinegar, sugar, salt and mirin in a jug and gently fold through the rice until well coated. Spread the rice evenly over a non-stick baking tray and allow to cool at room temperature.

4 Place one egg crepe on a sushi mat or a piece of greaseproof paper. Spread 4 tablespoons of the sushi rice over a third of the crepe, using a spatula or the back of a spoon.

5 Spread a tiny amount of wasabi along the centre of the rice, taking care when doing this as the wasabi is extremely hot. Place some tuna, cucumber, avocado and ginger over the wasabi.

6 Using the sushi mat or greaseproof paper to help you, fold the crepe over to enclose the filling and roll up firmly in the mat or paper. Cut the crepe roll into 2 cm (3/4 inch) rounds with a sharp knife. Serve with soy sauce.

COOKS FILE

Storage time: Sushi Crepes can be made in advance and stored in an airtight container in the fridge. Do not slice until serving—they may dry out.
Hint: If you find the rice sticking to your hands, keep them damp with a mixture of 2 teaspoons rice vinegar and 3 tablespoons water.
Note: Wasabi and pickled ginger are available in Asian grocery stores.

Cut the tuna, cucumber and avocado into even-sized matchsticks.

Pour sufficient egg mixture into a pan to lightly cover the base.

Cook the rice until small tunnels begin to appear on the surface.

Use a metal spoon to gently fold the dressing through the rice.

Spread 4 tablespoons of the rice over the bottom third of the crepe.

Roll the crepe up firmly using a sushi mat or greaseproof paper.

CRISPY ZUCCHINI CREPES WITH LIME DIP

Preparation time: 40 minutes
Total cooking time: 30–40 minutes
Serves 4

2 zucchini, cut into thin ribbons
    using a vegetable peeler
1/2 cup (60 g/2 oz) plain flour
pinch of salt
1 clove garlic, crushed
2 eggs
1 teaspoon sesame oil
1 teaspoon vegetable oil
3/4 cup (185 ml/6 fl oz) milk
1 1/2 tablespoons sesame seeds,
    toasted

Lime Yoghurt Dip
1 tablespoon lime juice
1 teaspoon ground cumin
200 ml (6 1/2 fl oz) Greek-style
    (thick) yoghurt

1 Blanch the zucchini ribbons in boiling water for 2 minutes, or until softened (don't overcook or they will fall apart). Drain well.
2 Sift the flour and salt into a bowl and make a well in the centre. Whisk together the garlic, eggs, oils, milk and sesame seeds in a jug; pour into the well and combine with the dry ingredients, whisking until the batter is just smooth. Fold in the blanched zucchini ribbons.
3 Preheat the oven to hot 220°C (425°F/Gas 7). Heat a small non-stick frying pan and brush lightly with oil. Pour 1/4 cup (60 ml/2 fl oz) batter into the pan and swirl gently to cover the base; use tongs to make the zucchini ribbons sit flat in the batter. Cook over medium heat for 1 minute, or until the underside is golden. Turn over and cook the other side until golden. Transfer to a plate and cover while cooking the remaining batter. Cut the crepes into thin wedges with a sharp knife and place on a non-stick baking tray. Brush the wedges lightly with oil and bake for 20 minutes or until crisp.
4 To make Lime Yoghurt Dip: Mix together the lime juice, cumin and yoghurt in a bowl. Serve the wedges with the Lime Yoghurt Dip, as part of an antipasto platter.

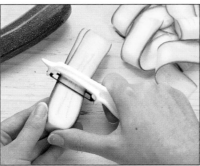

When preparing the ingredients, carefully peel each zucchini into thin ribbons.

Whisk the egg mixture into the flour until just smooth.

Use tongs to sit the zucchini ribbons flat in the pan.

Place the wedges on a non-stick baking tray and brush lightly with oil.

Add the liquid to the dry ingredients and whisk until just smooth.

Cut the spring onions in half lengthways and then blanch in boiling water.

Place the spring onions on top of the uncooked crepes in the pan.

SPRING ONION CREPES WITH CHINESE PORK

Preparation time: 20 minutes
Total cooking time: 10–15 minutes
Serves 4

1 cup (125 g/4 oz) plain flour
pinch of salt
2 eggs
30 g (1 oz) butter, melted
1 cup (250 ml/8 fl oz) milk
8 spring onions, cut into 12 cm (5 inch) lengths and halved lengthways
3 tablespoons hoisin sauce
500 g (1 lb) Chinese barbecued pork, shredded (see note)
¼ cup (7 g/¼ oz) coriander leaves

1 Sift the flour and a pinch of salt into a bowl and make a well in the centre. Whisk the eggs, butter and milk in a jug and pour into the well, whisking until just smooth and with the consistency of cream (this can be done in the food processor).
2 Lightly blanch the spring onions in boiling water for 2 minutes, or until they soften slightly, taking care not to let them discolour. Rinse under cold water and drain well.
3 Heat and lightly grease a crepe pan. Add enough batter, swirling gently, to coat the base; pour any excess back into the jug. Place a few spring onions in the batter (this needs to be done quickly or they won't cook as part of the crepe). Cook over medium heat for 1 minute, or until the underside is golden. Turn over and cook the other side. Transfer to a plate and cover to keep warm while cooking the remaining batter.
4 Place the crepes on a work surface, spring-onion-side down, and top with a little hoisin sauce, shredded pork and a few coriander leaves. Fold in the base, top and sides of the crepes to form little parcels.

Fill the crepes and fold them up neatly to form small parcels.

COOK'S FILE

Note: Buy barbecued pork at Chinese butchers. Ask the butcher to remove the bones and finely chop the meat.

SMOKED SALMON AND DILL CRESCENTS

Preparation time: 30 minutes
  + 30 minutes standing
Total cooking time: 15–20 minutes
Makes 64

3/4 cup (90 g/3 oz) plain flour
1 egg, plus 1 egg yolk
1 cup (250 ml/8 fl oz) milk
20 g (2/3 oz) butter, melted
2 tablespoons chopped fresh dill

Salmon Filling
1/2 cup (125 g/4 oz) sour cream
1 teaspoon grated onion
1 tablespoon horseradish cream
1 tablespoon mayonnaise
1 teaspoon lemon juice
2 tablespoons chopped fresh dill
100 g (3 1/3 oz) smoked salmon,
  chopped

1 Mix the flour, egg, yolk and half the milk in a food processor for 10 seconds, then add the remaining milk, butter and dill and continue to process until smooth. Pour the batter into a jug, cover and set aside for 30 minutes.

2 Heat a medium crepe pan and brush with melted butter. Pour about 1/4 cup (60 ml/2 fl oz) batter into the pan, swirling quickly to thinly cover the base. (Add a little more milk to the batter if it is too thick.) Pour any excess back into the jug. Cook the crepe for 30 seconds, then turn over and cook until lightly brown. Remove to a plate and cover with a tea towel while cooking the remaining batter.

3 To make Salmon Filling: Mix together the sour cream, onion, horseradish cream, mayonnaise,

lemon juice, dill and season with black pepper, to taste. Stir through the salmon. Spread each crepe with a heaped tablespoon of filling and cut into 8 triangles. Roll each triangle into a crescent shape, starting from the wide end. Cover and refrigerate until ready to serve.

Add the remaining milk, melted butter and dill to the food processor.

Mix all the ingredients for the Salmon Filling together.

Starting at the wide end, roll each triangle into a crescent shape.

CHICKEN CURRY BAGS

Preparation time: 30 minutes
  + 30 minutes standing
Total cooking time: 1 hour
Makes 10

1 cup (125 g/4 oz) plain flour
1 egg, plus 1 egg yolk
1¼ cups (315 ml/10 fl oz) milk
50 g (1⅔ oz) butter, melted
½ cup (60 g/2 oz) finely grated
    Cheddar cheese

Chicken Filling
1 large, cooked chicken breast
60 g (2 oz) butter
1 red onion, chopped
1–2 teaspoons curry powder
2 tablespoons plain flour
1¼ cups (315 ml/10 fl oz) milk
¼ cup (60 ml/2 fl oz) cream
¼ cup (15 g/½ oz) chopped
    fresh parsley
2 hard-boiled eggs, chopped

1 Mix the flour, egg, egg yolk and half the milk in a food processor for 10 seconds. Add the remaining milk and 1 tablespoon of the melted butter and process until the batter is smooth. Transfer to a jug, cover and set aside for 30 minutes.

2 To make Chicken Filling: Chop the cooked chicken into small cubes. Melt the butter in a pan, add the onion and cook over medium heat until softened. Add the curry powder and flour and cook for 1–2 minutes. Gradually add the milk, stirring until smooth. Cook for 2–3 minutes, or until the sauce has boiled and thickened. Remove from the heat and add the cream, chicken, parsley and egg. Cover and set aside.

3 Heat a small crepe pan and brush lightly with melted butter. Pour about ¼ cup (60 ml/2 fl oz) batter into the pan, swirling the pan to cover the base. Pour the excess batter back into the jug, adding a little more milk to the batter if it is too thick. Cook for about 30 seconds, then turn the crepe over and cook until lightly brown. Remove to a plate while cooking the remaining batter.

4 Preheat the oven to moderate 180°C (350°F/Gas 4). Place 3 tablespoons of Chicken Filling in the centre of each crepe then gather up into a bag. Tie loosely with a strip of foil, kitchen string or a couple of chives. Brush a large baking dish with melted butter, then brush each bag with melted butter and sprinkle with a little cheese. Bake for 10–15 minutes, or until the bags are heated and golden.

Remove from the heat and add the cream, chicken, parsley and chopped eggs.

Use a spatula to turn the crepe over and cook the other side.

Place 3 tablespoons of Chicken Filling in the centre of each crepe.

75

SPINACH AND RICOTTA CREPE CANNELLONI

Preparation time: 30 minutes
Total cooking time: 40–50 minutes
Serves 4

1 cup (150 g/4^3/4 oz) wholemeal
   plain flour
1 egg
1 cup (250 ml/8 fl oz) milk
1/2 cup (125 m/4 fl oz) plain
   yoghurt

Spinach and Ricotta Filling
500 g (1 lb) English spinach
   leaves, chopped
600 g (1 1/4 lb) fresh ricotta
1/2 teaspoon nutmeg
2 tablespoons chopped fresh
   basil
300 ml (9^2/3 fl oz) tomato pasta
   sauce
1/2 cup (125 g/4 oz) sour cream
1 cup (125 g/4 oz) grated
   Cheddar cheese

1 Preheat the oven to moderately hot 200°C (400°F/Gas 6). Sift the flour into a bowl and make a well in the centre. Whisk together the egg, milk and yoghurt in a jug and gradually pour into the well, whisking until just smooth. If the batter is very thick add a little more milk.

2 Heat a crepe pan and brush lightly with butter or oil. Add enough batter to the pan to thinly coat the base, pouring off any excess. Cook over medium heat for 1 minute, or until the underside is golden. Turn over and cook for 1 minute. Transfer to a plate and cover with a tea towel while cooking the remaining batter.

3 To make Spinach and Ricotta Filling: Steam the spinach until tender, then cool slightly and squeeze out the excess moisture with your hands. Mix with the ricotta, nutmeg and basil. Place 2 tablespoons of the filling along one edge of each crepe. Roll up the crepes to enclose the filling, leaving the ends open. Place in a lightly greased rectangular ovenproof dish.

4 Pour the pasta sauce over the crepes, top with dollops of sour cream and sprinkle with cheese. Bake for 30 minutes, or until crisp and golden.

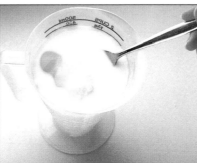

Use a fork to whisk the egg, milk and yoghurt together in a jug.

Turn the crepe over when it is golden and cook the other side.

Use your hands to squeeze the excess moisture from the steamed spinach.

Carefully roll up the crepes to enclose the Spinach and Ricotta Filling.

POPPY SEED CREPES WITH SEAFOOD FILLING

Preparation time: 50 minutes
    + 30 minutes standing
Total cooking time: 30 minutes
Serves 8

1 cup (125 g/4 oz) plain flour
1 egg, plus 1 egg yolk
1 cup (250 ml/8 fl oz) milk
20 g (2/3 oz) butter, melted
1 tablespoon poppy seeds

Seafood Filling
1 cup (250 ml/8 fl oz) white
    wine
1/2 cup (125 ml/4 fl oz) fish
    stock or water
200 g (6 1/2 oz) small scallops
400 g (12 2/3 oz) raw prawns,
    peeled, deveined and halved
200 g (6 1/2 oz) boneless white
    fish fillets
60 g (2 oz) butter
3 spring onions, chopped
2 bacon rashers, chopped
1/4 cup (30 g/1 oz) plain flour
3/4 cup (185 ml/6 fl oz) cream
1 teaspoon lemon juice
1/4 cup (15 g/1/2 oz) fresh
    parsley, chopped
2 tablespoons chopped chives

1 Mix the flour, egg, egg yolk and half the milk in a food processor for 10 seconds. Add the remaining milk, butter and poppy seeds and process until smooth. Pour into a jug, cover, and set aside for 30 minutes. Heat a crepe pan and brush lightly with melted butter. Add enough batter to thinly cover the base, pouring the excess back into the jug. Cook for 30 seconds, turn over and cook until lightly brown. Remove and cover while cooking the remaining batter.

2 To make Seafood Filling: Heat the wine and stock or water in a pan until simmering. Add the seafood and cook for 4 minutes. Drain, reserving the liquid. Flake the fish. Melt the butter in a pan, add the spring onions and bacon and stir for 2–3 minutes, or until cooked. Add the flour and stir for 1 minute. Add 1 cup (250 ml/ 8 fl oz) of the reserved stock and stir for 2 minutes, or until thickened. Stir in the cream, lemon juice, some pepper, parsley and chives. Add the seafood and heat gently for 2–3 minutes, taking care not to overcook.

3 Place 2 tablespoons of filling over a quarter of each crepe. Fold the crepes in half and then quarters to serve.

COOK'S FILE

Note: Crepes and filling can both be made several hours in advance.

Add the remaining milk, butter and poppy seeds to the food processor.

Pour sufficient batter into the pan to thinly coat the base.

Add the drained seafood to the sauce and then heat gently.

CHEESE AND SPINACH BUCKWHEAT CREPES

Preparation time: 35 minutes +
  30 minutes standing
Total cooking time: 40–50 minutes
Makes about 10

1 cup (130 g/4^1/$_4$ oz) buckwheat
  flour
2 eggs
1^1/$_4$ cups (315 ml/10 fl oz) milk
30 g (1 oz) butter, melted

Cheese and Spinach Filling
500 g (1 lb) English Spinach
40 g (1^1/$_3$ oz) butter
1 small red onion, chopped
1 small red capsicum, chopped
1–2 cloves garlic, crushed
2 bacon rashers, chopped
375 g (12 oz) fresh ricotta
^{1}/$_4$ cup (60 ml/2 fl oz) cream
^{1}/$_2$ teaspoon nutmeg

1 Mix the buckwheat flour, eggs and half the milk in a food processor for 10 seconds, add the remaining milk and butter and process until smooth. Pour into a jug, cover and set aside for 30 minutes. Heat a medium crepe or frying pan and brush lightly with melted butter. Pour about ^{1}/$_4$ cup (60 ml/2 fl oz) batter into the pan, swirling to thinly cover the base. Pour the excess batter back into the jug. (Add a little more milk to batter if it is too thick.) Cook for 1 minute. Turn the crepe over and cook the other side until lightly brown. Remove and cover with a tea towel while cooking the remaining batter.

2 To make Cheese and Spinach Filling: Remove the stalks and wash the spinach in cold water. Place in a large pan, cover and cook until wilted. Drain and cool. Squeeze the moisture from the spinach, chop and place in a bowl. Heat half the butter in a pan, add the onion, capsicum, garlic and bacon and cook for 5 minutes, or until softened. Cool and add to the spinach. Stir in the ricotta, cream, nutmeg and season with pepper.

3 Preheat the oven to moderate 180°C (350°F/Gas 4). Spread each crepe with 2 heaped tablespoons of filling. Fold the crepes in half, then into quarters. Arrange in overlapping rows in a greased baking dish, brush lightly with the remaining melted butter, cover with foil and bake 15 minutes, or until heated through.

Add the remaining milk and butter to the food processor.

Add the ricotta, cream, nutmeg and some pepper, and stir well.

Spread the crepes with filling, fold in half and then into quarters.

SALMON AND DILL PINWHEELS

Preparation time: 30 minutes
+ 30 minutes standing
Total cooking time: 20 minutes
Makes about 35 slices

1 cup (125 g/4 oz) self-raising
flour
1/2 cup (75 g/2½ oz) wholemeal
self-raising flour
2 eggs
1¾ cups (440 ml/14 fl oz) milk
50 g (1²/3 oz) butter, melted

Salmon and Dill Filling
210 g (6³/4 oz) can red salmon,
drained
125 g (4 oz) light cream cheese,
at room temperature
1/2 cup (125 g/4 oz) sour cream
1 teaspoon grated lemon rind
2 teaspoons lemon juice
4 spring onions, finely chopped
1/4 cup (15 g/1/2 oz) finely
chopped fresh dill

1 Mix the combined flours, eggs and half the milk in a food processor for 10 seconds. Add the remaining milk and butter and process until smooth. Pour into a jug, cover and set aside for 30 minutes.

2 Heat a medium crepe or frying pan and brush lightly with melted butter. Pour enough batter into the pan to thinly cover the base and pour the excess back into the jug. (Add a little more milk if the batter is too thick.) Cook for 1 minute, turn over and cook until lightly brown. Remove and cook the remaining batter.

3 To make Salmon and Dill Filling: Mash the salmon with a fork,

then add the cream cheese, sour cream, lemon rind and juice. Mix until smooth, then fold in the spring onions and dill. Spread a tablespoonful of

filling over each crepe. Stack 3 crepes on top of each other and roll up firmly. Trim the ends with a sharp knife then cut into slices to serve.

Swirl the pan quickly to thinly cover the base with batter.

Fold the spring onions and dill through the salmon mixture.

Spread the crepes with filling and then roll up in stacks of three.

CHIVE CREPE CORNETS WITH SMOKED TROUT

Preparation time: 45 minutes
  + 30 minutes standing
Total cooking time: 15–20 minutes
Makes 20

3/4 cup (90 g/3 oz) plain flour
1 egg, plus 1 egg yolk
1 cup (250 ml/8 fl oz) milk
20 g (2/3 oz) butter, melted
2 tablespoons chopped chives

Smoked Trout Filling
250 g (8 oz) smoked trout
125 g (4 oz) cream cheese, at
    room temperature
1/4 cup (60 g/2 oz) sour cream
1/4 cup (60 ml/2 fl oz) cream
Tabasco sauce
2 teaspoons lemon juice
1 tablespoon chopped chives
1 tablespoon chopped capers
2 small gherkins, finely
    chopped
1 carrot, cut into julienne strips
    (see note)
1 celery stalk, cut into julienne
    strips
extra chives

1 Mix the flour, egg and egg yolk and half the milk in a food processor. Process for 10 seconds, then add the remaining milk and butter and process until smooth. Pour into a jug, cover and set aside for 30 minutes.
2 Heat a medium crepe or frying pan and brush lightly with melted butter. Pour enough batter into the pan to thinly cover the base, pouring the excess back into the jug. (Add more milk to the batter if it is too thick.)

Sprinkle the batter with chives and cook for about 30 seconds. Turn the crepe over and cook the other side until lightly brown. Transfer to a plate while cooking the remaining batter and chives.
2 To make Smoked Trout Filling: Remove the skin from the trout. Carefully lift the flesh from bones, keeping it as intact as possible and removing any stray bones. Divide into twenty even-sized pieces. Mix together the cream cheese, sour cream, cream, a few drops of Tabasco, lemon juice, chopped chives, capers and gherkins. Place the carrot and celery in boiling water and blanch for 1 minute, then cool in cold water. Drain and dry on paper towels.
3 Place a crepe on the work surface, chive-side-down. Spread with the cream cheese filling mixture, then cut in half. Fold each half-crepe in half, so that the chives show decoratively. Repeat with the remaining crepes.
4 Arrange a piece of trout, a few sticks of carrot and celery, and 2–3 sprigs of chives on each folded crepe, then roll up firmly like a cornet. The julienned vegetables should poke decoratively from the top of the crepe. Fold the top edge of each cornet over (you could use a little remaining filling to make them stick). Cover and refrigerate until ready to serve.

COOK'S FILE

Note: Julienne strips are even-sized pieces of vegetables, about the width of a matchstick. Because of their size, they do not require much cooking—usually just blanching—and look very decorative. Cut them using a sharp knife. It can be time-consuming, but is worth it for the effect.

Cut the vegetables into julienne strips with a sharp knife.

Mix the flour, egg, egg yolk and half the milk in a food processor.

Cover the base of the pan with batter, then sprinkle with chopped chives.

80

Carefully peel away the skin from the smoked trout.

Carefully lift the bones from the trout, keeping the flesh intact.

Combine the ingredients for the cream cheese mixture.

OLIVE WEDGES WITH CAPSICUM PESTO

Preparation time: 10 minutes
Total cooking time: 10 minutes
Serves 6

1 cup (125 g/4 oz) plain flour
1 egg
1¹/2 cups (375 ml/12 fl oz) milk
200 g (6¹/2 oz) marinated
    Kalamata olives, sliced
1 small red chilli, finely
    chopped
Parmesan shavings, to garnish
2 tablespoons shredded basil

Sun-dried Capsicum Pesto
200 g (6¹/2 oz) sun-dried
    capsicum, drained
¹/4 cup (40 g/1¹/3 oz) pine nuts
2 tablespoons freshly grated
    Parmesan cheese

1 Sift the flour into a large bowl and make a well in the centre. Whisk the egg and milk in a jug and gradually pour into the well, whisking until just smooth. Transfer the batter to a jug and stir in the olives and chilli.

2 Heat a crepe or frying pan and brush lightly with melted butter. Add ¹/3 cup (80 ml/2³/4 fl oz) batter and cook over medium heat for 1 minute, or until the underside is golden. Turn over and cook the other side until golden. Remove the crepe and cover with a tea towel while cooking the remaining batter.

3 To make Sun-dried Capsicum Pesto: Mix the sun-dried capsicum, pine nuts and Parmesan in a food processor until smooth.

4 Place the crepes, olive-side-up, on a board. Spread all but one of the crepes with three-quarters of the Sun-dried Capsicum Pesto. Stack the crepes on top of each other, finishing with the plain crepe. Top with the remaining pesto. Garnish with shavings of Parmesan, fresh basil and cracked black pepper.

COOK'S FILE

Note: This dish is delicious hot or cold and makes a great addition to any picnic basket.

Variation: Use sun-dried tomatoes instead of capsicum if you prefer.

Stir the sliced olives and chopped chilli into the batter.

When the underside is golden, turn the crepe over and cook the other side.

Place all the Pesto ingredients in a food processor and mix until smooth.

Spread all but one of the crepes with Sun-dried Capsicum Pesto.

CREPE MONEY BAGS WITH SATAY PORK

Preparation time: 40 minutes
Total cooking time: 30–35 minutes
Serves 4

Pork Filling
1 teaspoon sesame oil
1 teaspoon peanut oil
1 clove garlic, crushed
1 tablespoon grated fresh ginger
1 small red chilli, finely
  chopped
250 g (8 oz) minced pork
230 g (7$^1/_3$ oz) can water
  chestnuts, chopped
1 tablespoon peanut butter
1 teaspoon lime juice
1 teaspoon fish sauce
6 chives, blanched

1 cup (150 g/4$^3/_4$ oz) wholemeal
  plain flour
1 egg
30 g (1 oz) butter, melted
1$^1/_2$ cups (375 ml/12 fl oz)
  buttermilk

1 To make Pork Filling: Heat the sesame oil and peanut oil in a frying pan, add the garlic, ginger and chilli and cook over medium heat for 3 minutes. Add the pork and cook over high heat, stirring to break up any lumps, until browned. Add the water chestnuts, peanut butter, lime juice and fish sauce and cook for 3 minutes, or until heated through. Remove from the heat and allow to cool slightly.

2 Sift the flour and a pinch of salt into a bowl, returning the husks, and make a well in the centre. Whisk the egg, butter and buttermilk in a jug

and gradually pour into the well, whisking until just smooth (this may also be done in a food processor).

3 Heat a crepe or frying pan and brush lightly with melted butter. Add $^1/_4$ cup (60 ml/2 fl oz) batter to cover the base of the pan. Cook over medium heat for 1 minute, or until the underside is golden. Turn over and

cook for 1 minute, or until golden. Remove and cover while cooking the remaining batter, greasing the pan when necessary.

4 Divide the filling among the crepes and gather up the edges to make bags. Tie a chive around each bag to hold it together—don't pull too tight or it may break. Serve immediately.

Add the water chestnuts, peanut butter, lime juice and fish sauce to the mince.

Sift the flour into a bowl and then return the husks.

Add the batter to the pan and swirl so it thinly covers the base.

WAFFLES

WAFFLES WITH HOT CHOCOLATE SAUCE

Preparation time: 20 minutes
Total cooking time: 15–20 minutes
Makes 8 waffles

2 cups (250 g/8 oz) self-raising
  flour
1 teaspoon bicarbonate
  of soda
2 teaspoons sugar
2 eggs
140 g (4²/3 oz) butter
1³/4 cups (440 ml/14 fl oz)
  buttermilk
200 g (6¹/2 oz) dark chocolate,
  chopped
¹/2 cup (125 ml/4 fl oz) cream
1 tablespoon golden syrup

1 Preheat the waffle iron. Sift the flour, soda, sugar and a pinch of salt into a large bowl and make a well in the centre. Whisk the eggs, 90 g (3 oz) melted butter and the buttermilk in a jug and gradually pour into the well, whisking until just smooth. Set the batter aside for 10 minutes.
2 Put the remaining butter, chocolate, cream and syrup in a pan and stir over low heat until smooth. Remove from the heat and keep warm.
3 Brush the waffle iron with melted butter. Pour ¹/2 cup (125 ml/4 fl oz) of batter into the centre and spread almost to the corners of the grid.
4 Close the lid and cook for 2 minutes or until golden and crisp. Keep warm while cooking the remaining mixture. Serve with vanilla ice cream and the hot chocolate sauce.

Gradually add the liquid to the well in the centre of the dry ingredients.

Combine the remaining butter, chocolate, cream and syrup in a pan.

Pour ¹/2 cup of the batter into the heated waffle iron.

Cook the waffle for about 2 minutes, or until golden and crisp.

GINGERBREAD WAFFLES

Preparation time: 20 minutes
Total cooking time: 35 minutes
Makes 8 waffles

125 g (4 oz) butter
1/2 cup (125 g/4 oz) sugar
2 eggs
1/2 cup (175 g/5²/3 oz) molasses
2 cups (250 g/8 oz) plain flour
1 teaspoon ground cinnamon
1/2 teaspoon ground nutmeg
1 1/2 teaspoons ground ginger
1/2 teaspoon ground cloves
1 1/2 teaspoons bicarbonate of
    soda
1/2 teaspoon salt
1/2 cup (125 ml/4 fl oz) boiling
    water
maple syrup, to serve

1 Preheat the waffle iron. Beat the butter and sugar together in a small bowl until light and creamy. Beat in the eggs one at a time, then add the molasses and beat until combined. Transfer the mixture to a large bowl. Sift together the flour, cinnamon, nutmeg, ginger, cloves, bicarbonate of soda and salt and fold in, alternately with the water.

2 Brush both surfaces of the heated waffle iron with melted butter. Pour a generous 1/2 cup (125 ml/4 fl oz) of the batter into the centre of the waffle iron and spread almost to the corners of the grid. Cook until golden and crisp (this should take approximately 4–5 minutes). Remove from the iron and keep warm while cooking the remaining mixture.

3 Waffles are best served hot. Drizzle with maple syrup and perhaps serve with ice cream and fresh fruit.

Beat the butter and sugar together in a small bowl until light and creamy.

Fold in the sifted dry ingredients, alternately with the water.

Brush both the grids of the waffle iron with melted butter.

BERRY WAFFLES

Preparation time: 30 minutes
Total cooking time: 20 minutes
Serves 4

1¹/2 cups (185 g/6 oz) self-
    raising flour
2 eggs
2 tablespoons sugar
30 g (1 oz) butter, melted
125 g (4 oz) fresh ricotta
1 cup (250 ml/8 fl oz) milk
500 g (1 lb) mixed berries

Strawberry Butter
250 g (8 oz) unsalted butter,
    softened
1/2 cup (60 g/2 oz) icing sugar
200 g (6¹/2 oz) strawberries,
    hulled

1 Preheat the waffle iron. Sift the flour into a bowl and make a well in the centre. Whisk the eggs, sugar, melted butter, ricotta and milk in a jug and gradually pour into the well, whisking until just smooth.

2 Brush both surfaces of the heated waffle iron with melted butter. Pour ¹/2 cup (125 ml/4 fl oz) of batter into the centre of the waffle iron and spread almost to the corners of the grid. Close the waffle iron and cook for 5 minutes, or until the waffles are crisp and golden. Keep warm while cooking the remaining mixture.

3 To make Strawberry Butter: Beat the butter and icing sugar together until light and creamy. Purée the strawberries in a food processor, then beat into the creamed mixture. Arrange the waffles on a plate, top with a little Strawberry Butter and serve with mixed fresh berries.

Whisk together the eggs, sugar, melted butter, ricotta and milk with a fork.

Pour the liquid into the well in the centre of the dry ingredients.

Beat the strawberry purée through the whipped butter mixture.

BUTTERMILK WAFFLES WITH RHUBARB AND CINNAMON CREAM

Preparation time: 25 minutes
Total cooking time: 30 minutes
Serves 4

1 bunch rhubarb, chopped
1/2 cup (125 g/4 oz) caster sugar
1 cup (150 g/4³/4 oz) wholemeal
    self-raising flour
1 cup (125 g/4 oz) plain flour
2 teaspoons baking powder
3 tablespoons soft brown sugar
2 eggs
100 g (3¹/3 oz) butter, melted

1³/4 cups (440 ml/14 fl oz)
    buttermilk
1 tablespoon grated orange rind

Cinnamon Cream
300 ml (9²/3 fl oz) cream
1 teaspoon vanilla essence
1 teaspoon ground cinnamon

1 Place the rhubarb, sugar and 1/2 cup (125 ml/4 fl oz) water in a large pan and stir over low heat until the sugar dissolves. Bring to the boil, reduce the heat and simmer for 7–10 minutes, or until the rhubarb is very soft and beginning to fall apart.

2 Preheat the waffle iron. Sift the flours and baking powder into a bowl,

returning the husks. Stir in the brown sugar and make a well in the centre. Mix together the eggs, butter, buttermilk and rind and pour into the well, whisking until just smooth. (Add a little milk if the batter is too thick.)

3 Brush both surfaces of the waffle iron with melted butter. Spoon 1/2 cup (125 ml/4 fl oz) batter into the centre of the waffle iron and spread almost to the corners of the grid. Close the waffle iron and cook for 3–5 minutes, or until the waffle is crisp and golden. Keep warm while cooking the rest.

4 To make Cinnamon Cream: Beat the cream, vanilla essence and cinnamon until soft peaks form. Serve with the waffles and rhubarb.

Simmer the rhubarb until it has softened and is beginning to fall apart.

Add the buttermilk mixture to the well in the centre of the dry ingredients.

Cook the waffle for 3–5 minutes, or until crisp and golden.

Whisk the eggs, vanilla essence, soy milk and butter together in a jug.

Brush both surfaces of the waffle iron with melted butter.

MACADAMIA WAFFLES WITH BUTTERSCOTCH BANANAS

Preparation time: 35 minutes
Total cooking time: 30 minutes
Serves 4

2 cups (250 g/8 oz) plain flour
2 teaspoons baking powder
125 g (4 oz) macadamia nuts, roasted and roughly chopped
1/4 cup (45 g/1 1/2 oz) soft brown sugar
2 eggs
1 teaspoon vanilla essence
1 3/4 cups (440 ml/14 fl oz) soy milk
50 g (1 2/3 oz) butter, melted
150 ml (4 3/4 fl oz) pure thick cream

Butterscotch Bananas
50 g (1 2/3 oz) butter
1/2 cup (95 g/3 1/4 oz) soft brown sugar
1 tablespoon brandy
300 ml (9 1/2 fl oz) cream
4 bananas, halved lengthways

1 Preheat the waffle iron. Sift the flour and baking powder into a bowl, add the macadamia nuts and brown sugar and make a well in the centre. Whisk the eggs, vanilla essence, soy milk and butter in a jug and gradually pour into the well, whisking until the batter is just smooth.
2 Brush both surfaces of the heated waffle iron with melted butter. Pour 1/2 cup (125 ml/4 fl oz) of the batter into the centre and spread almost to the corners of the grid. Close the iron and cook for 4 minutes, or until the waffle is crisp and golden brown. Remove and keep warm while cooking the remaining batter.
3 **To make Butterscotch Bananas:** Melt the butter in a frying pan over medium heat. Stir in the brown sugar and cook for 3 minutes, or until the sugar has dissolved. Stir in the brandy and cream, bring to the boil, reduce the heat and simmer for 3 minutes. Add the bananas and cook for 2 minutes, or until they soften slightly.
4 Cut the waffles into wedges and serve with thick cream and the Butterscotch Bananas.

Use the back of a spoon to spread the batter almost to the corners of the iron.

Carefully add the bananas to the hot butterscotch sauce.

COOK'S FILE

Hint: Any nuts may be used in place of the macadamias. Try apples or pears as an alternative to bananas.

YOGHURT PISTACHIO WAFFLES WITH LEMON BLUEBERRIES

Preparation time: 35 minutes
Total cooking time: 20–30 minutes
Serves 4

Lemon Blueberries
300 g (9²/3 oz) fresh blueberries
1¹/3 cups (350 ml/11 fl oz)
    water
1 cinnamon stick
¹/4 cup (90 g/3 oz) golden syrup
2 tablespoons soft brown sugar
1 teaspoon grated lemon rind
plain yoghurt, to serve

1 cup (125 g/4 oz) plain flour
1 cup (125 g/4 oz) self-raising
    flour
2 tablespoons caster sugar
¹/2 teaspoon nutmeg
100 g (3¹/3 oz) finely chopped
    pistachio nuts
600 g (1¹/4 lb) honey yoghurt
2 eggs, separated
60 g (2 oz) butter, melted

1 To make Lemon Blueberries: Place the blueberries, water and cinnamon stick in a small pan. Simmer over low heat for 15 minutes. Remove and discard the cinnamon stick. Add the golden syrup, brown sugar and lemon rind to the berries in the pan and stir gently until the sugar has dissolved and the mixture is combined. Set aside to cool.
2 Preheat the waffle iron. Sift the flours into a large bowl. Add the sugar, nutmeg and pistachio nuts and make a well in the centre. Whisk together the yoghurt, egg yolks and butter in a jug and then slowly pour into the well, whisking the batter until just smooth.
3 In a small dry bowl, beat the egg whites with electric beaters until firm peaks form.
4 Stir a tablespoon of the beaten egg whites into the batter to loosen it up. Gently and thoroughly fold the remaining egg whites into the batter.
5 Brush both surfaces of the heated waffle iron with melted butter. Pour approximately ¹/2 cup (125 ml/4 fl oz) of batter into the centre of the waffle iron and spread almost to the corners of the grid.
6 Close the lid and cook the waffle for about 3–4 minutes, or until golden. Remove the waffle from the iron and keep warm while cooking the remaining batter. Spoon the Lemon Blueberries over the top of the waffles and serve with a spoonful of yoghurt.

COOK'S FILE

Hint: If you want to crisp waffles, toast them under a grill or in a toaster.
Note: To make your own yoghurt, use 2 cups (500 ml/16 fl oz) of either skim or full-cream milk. Put the milk in a pan, bring to the boil until the froth rises and then reduce the heat and simmer gently for at least 2 minutes. Leave to cool until lukewarm (about 43–44°C/110–115°F). Blend about 2 tablespoons natural yoghurt with a little of the warm milk and then stir into the rest of the milk. Pour into a warmed Pyrex bowl or sterilised jars and seal tightly. Leave the yoghurt in a warm place for at least 6 hours (you may need to wrap a cloth around the jars), or until cooled and set. Refrigerate the yoghurt for about 2 hours before using.

Add the golden syrup, brown sugar and lemon rind to the berries.

Add the sugar, nutmeg and pistachio nuts to the flour.

Beat the egg whites in a small dry bowl until firm peaks form.

Use a metal spoon to fold the remaining egg whites through the batter.

Spread the batter almost to the corners of the waffle iron grid.

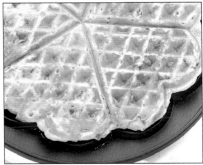
Close the lid and cook the waffle for 3–4 minutes, or until crisp and golden.

BANANA OATMEAL WAFFLES WITH HONEYED YOGHURT

Preparation time: 20 minutes
Total cooking time: 25 minutes
Makes 5 waffles

1 cup (250 g/8 oz) plain yoghurt
1/4 cup(60 ml/2 fl oz) orange
    juice
2 tablespoons honey
1 teaspoon grated lemon rind
1/2 teaspoon fresh grated ginger
3/4 cup (75 g/2 1/2 oz) rolled oats
2/3 cup (85 g/2 3/4 oz) plain flour
1 teaspoon baking powder
1/2 teaspoon bicarbonate of soda
2 eggs
3/4 cup (185 ml/6 fl oz) milk
2 tablespoons oil
1 teaspoon vanilla essence
1 ripe banana, mashed

1 Mix together the yoghurt, orange juice, honey, rind and ginger in a bowl. Cover and refrigerate.
2 Preheat the waffle iron. Mix together the oats, flour, baking powder and bicarbonate of soda in a bowl and make a well in the centre. Whisk the eggs, milk, oil and vanilla in a jug; add the banana and beat until combined. Pour into the well, whisking until just smooth.
3 Brush the waffle iron with melted butter. Pour 1/2 cup (125 ml/4 fl oz) of batter into the centre of the waffle iron and spread almost to the corners of the grid. Cook for 4–5 minutes, or until golden and crisp. Keep warm while cooking the remaining batter. Serve the waffles warm with the honeyed yoghurt, garnished with fresh banana.

Add the mashed banana to the combined eggs, milk, oil and vanilla essence.

Add the banana mixture to the well in the dry ingredients and whisk to combine.

Pour a generous 1/2 cup of batter into the centre of the waffle iron.

92

MOCHA WAFFLES WITH ESPRESSO SYRUP

Preparation time: 30 minutes
Total cooking time: 30–40 minutes
Makes 8 waffles

Espresso Syrup
3/4 cup (185 g/6 oz) caster sugar
1/2 cup (125 ml/4 fl oz) brewed
   espresso coffee
1/4 cup (60 ml/2 fl oz) cream

2 cups (250 g/8 oz) plain flour
2 tablespoons cocoa powder
2 teaspoons baking powder
1/2 teaspoon salt
1 1/4 cups (315 ml/10 fl oz) milk
2 tablespoons coffee and chicory
   essence
1/2 cup (125 g/4 oz) caster sugar
3 eggs, separated
60 g (2 oz) butter, melted

1 To make Espresso Syrup: Put the sugar, espresso coffee, cream and 3 tablespoonsful of water in a small pan. Bring to the boil, reduce the heat and simmer for 4–5 minutes. Set aside to cool.

2 Preheat the waffle iron. Sift the flour, cocoa, baking powder and salt into a large bowl. Add the milk, essence, sugar, egg yolks and butter and whisk until smooth. In a clean dry bowl, beat the egg whites until firm peaks form. Stir a tablespoon of egg white into the batter to loosen it up, then gently fold in the remainder.

3 Brush the waffle iron with melted butter. Pour 1/2 cup (125 ml/4 fl oz) of batter into the centre of the iron and spread almost to the corners of the grid. Cook for about 4–5 minutes, or until crisp and golden. Keep warm while cooking the remaining batter. Spoon Espresso Syrup over the waffles. Delicious served with freshly whipped cream, chocolate curls and a sifting of cocoa powder.

Combine the sugar, espresso coffee, cream and water in a pan.

Whisk the combined milk, essence, sugar, yolks and butter into the dry ingredients.

Using the back of a spoon, spread the batter almost to the corners of the iron.

93

ORANGE AND PASSIONFRUIT WAFFLES WITH LEMON CURD

Preparation time: 40 minutes
Total cooking time: 45 minutes
Makes 4–6

Lemon Curd
4 eggs
3/4 cup (185 g/6 oz) caster sugar
2 teaspoons grated lemon rind
1/2 cup (125 ml/4 fl oz) lemon
   juice
125 g (4 oz) butter, chopped

2 cups (250 g/8 oz) plain flour
1/2 teaspoon baking powder
1/3 cup (90 g/3 oz) caster sugar
1 tablespoon grated orange rind
2 eggs, separated
1 cup (250 ml/8 fl oz) milk
1/2 cup (125 g/4 oz) passionfruit
   pulp
60 g (2 oz) butter, melted

1 **To make Lemon Curd:** Place the eggs, sugar, rind, juice, butter and 3 tablespoons water in a heatproof bowl and place over a smaller pan of simmering water. Stir or whisk until the Lemon Curd mixture coats the back of a metal spoon. Remove from the heat, cover and refrigerate until ready to use.
2 Preheat the waffle iron. Sift the flour and baking powder into a bowl. Add the sugar and orange rind and make a well in the centre. Whisk the egg yolks, milk, passionfruit pulp and melted butter in a jug. Gradually pour into the well, whisking until the batter is just smooth.
3 Beat the egg whites in a small dry bowl until firm peaks form (any grease on the bowl will prevent the eggs aerating). Stir a tablespoon of the egg white into the batter to loosen it up, then gently fold in the remainder.
4 Brush both surfaces of the waffle iron with melted butter. Pour 1/2 cup (125 ml/4 fl oz) batter into the centre of the waffle iron and spread almost to the corners of the grid. Close the lid and cook for about 1–2 minutes, or until the waffle is crisp and golden. Transfer to a plate while cooking the remaining batter. Serve with the Lemon Curd and ice cream.

Put all the ingredients for Lemon Curd in a heatproof bowl on top of a pan.

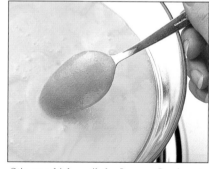

Stir or whisk until the Lemon Curd coats the back of a metal spoon.

With a fork, whisk the egg yolks, milk, passionfruit and melted butter in a jug.

Beat the egg whites in a clean, dry bowl until firm peaks form.

Mix the hazelnuts and butter in a food processor until smooth.

Wrap the butter in a sheet of foil to form a cylinder shape.

Use a metal spoon to gently fold the firm egg white into the batter.

Cook the waffle for 2–3 minutes, or until crisp and golden.

SOUR CREAM WAFFLES WITH HAZELNUT BUTTER AND RASPBERRIES

Preparation time: 35 minutes
Total cooking time: 20 minutes
Makes 4 waffles

Hazelnut Butter
125 g (4 oz) butter, softened
60 g (2 oz) roasted hazelnuts, skinned

2 cups (250 g/8 oz) plain flour
1 teaspoon baking powder
2 tablespoons caster sugar
3 eggs, separated
1½ cups (375 g/12 oz) sour cream
1 cup (250 ml/8 fl oz) milk
1 teaspoon vanilla essence
60 g (2 oz) butter, melted
300 g (9²/3 oz) fresh raspberries, to serve

1 To make Hazelnut Butter: Mix the butter and hazelnuts in a food processor until smooth. Scrape the butter onto a sheet of foil and wrap into a cylinder shape, twisting the ends tightly. Refrigerate until firm. To serve, unwrap and cut into thin slices.
2 Preheat the waffle iron. Sift the flour and baking powder into a bowl, add the sugar and make a well in the centre. Whisk the egg yolks, sour cream, milk, vanilla and butter in a jug and gradually pour into the well, whisking until just smooth.
3 Beat the egg whites in a small bowl with electric beaters until firm peaks form. Stir a tablespoon of the egg white into the batter to loosen it up, then gently fold in the remainder.
4 Brush both surfaces of the waffle iron with melted butter. Pour ½ cup (125 ml/4 fl oz) batter into the centre of the waffle iron and spread almost to the corners of the grid. Close the lid and cook for about 2–3 minutes, or

until golden. Remove the waffle from the iron and keep warm while cooking the remaining batter. Serve with Hazelnut Butter and raspberries.

LIQUEUR ORANGES WITH ZESTY MARMALADE WAFFLES

Preparation time: 35 minutes
+ 1–2 hours refrigeration
Total cooking time: 30–40 minutes
Makes 8 waffles

Liqueur Oranges
6 oranges
1/2 cup (125 ml/4 fl oz) orange juice
1/2 cup (125 g/4 oz) caster sugar
2 tablespoons Cointreau

1 1/2 cups (185 g/6 oz) plain flour, sifted
1 1/2 teaspoons baking powder
1/2 teaspoon salt
1 tablespoon soft brown sugar
1 cup (250 ml/8 fl oz) milk
3 eggs
60 g (2 oz) butter, melted
3/4 cup (240 g/7 1/2 oz) orange marmalade
1/2 cup (80 g/2 2/3 oz) almonds, toasted, finely chopped

1 To make Liqueur Oranges: Using a sharp knife, cut off all the skin and pith right to the flesh of each orange. Slice the flesh thinly, discarding any seeds, and set aside. Place the orange juice and sugar in a small pan and stir until the sugar has dissolved. Bring to the boil, then stir in the liqueur and leave to cool. Once cooled, add the sliced oranges. Cover and put in the refrigerator for a minimum of 1–2 hours.
2 Preheat the waffle iron. Sift the flour, baking powder and salt into a bowl. Stir in the brown sugar and make a well in the centre. Whisk the milk, eggs, butter and marmalade in a jug and gradually pour into the well, whisking until just smooth. Add the almonds and mix well.
3 Brush both surfaces of the heated waffle iron with melted butter. Pour 1/2 cup (125 ml/4 fl oz) batter into the centre of the waffle iron and spread almost to the edge of the grid. Close the lid and cook for 4–5 minutes, or until golden and crisp. Keep warm while cooking the remaining mixture. Serve warm with Liqueur Oranges, ice cream or cream.

Peel the skin and pith from the oranges and thinly slice the flesh.

Add the almonds to the waffle batter and stir well.

Pour the batter onto the waffle iron and spread almost to the edge.

MUESLI WAFFLES WITH FRUIT COMPOTE

Preparation time: 20 minutes
 + 30 minutes marinating
Total cooking time: 15–20 minutes
Makes 6

Fruit Compote
500 g (1 lb) strawberries, hulled
 and quartered
1 ripe papaya, peeled and diced
2 firm kiwi fruit, peeled and
 diced
2 tablespoons honey

1 cup (125 g/4 oz) plain flour
1 cup (150 g/4³/4 oz) wholemeal
 plain flour
1/2 teaspoon baking powder
1 cup (110 g/3²/3 oz) natural
 muesli
3 eggs, separated
1¹/2 cups (375 ml/12 fl oz) milk
60 g (2 oz) butter, melted

1 To make Fruit Compote: Put the fruit in a large bowl, drizzle with the honey, cover and set aside at room temperature for 30 minutes.
2 Preheat the waffle iron. Sift the flours and baking powder into a bowl

and return the husks. Add the muesli and make a well in the centre. Whisk the egg yolks, milk and butter in a jug and pour into the well, stirring until just smooth. Beat the egg whites until firm peaks form. Stir a tablespoon of egg white into the batter to loosen it, then gently fold in the remainder.
3 Brush both surfaces of the waffle iron with melted butter. Pour 1/2 cup (125 ml/4 fl oz) batter into the centre and spread almost to the corners of the grid. Cook for 1–2 minutes, or until golden and crisp. Keep warm while cooking the remainder. Serve with the Fruit Compote.

Add the muesli to the sifted flours and baking powder.

Add the egg mixture to the well in the centre of the dry ingredients.

Using a metal spoon, gently fold in the remaining beaten egg white.

QUICK WAFFLE DESSERTS

When friends drop in unexpectedly and the cupboard is bare, waffles make wonderful emergency desserts. Either make up plain waffles from the basic recipe on page 85 (these can be frozen for up to 1 month—thaw them quickly, or toast to thaw, so they don't become soggy) or, if you don't have a waffle maker, use one of the many varieties of shop-bought waffles.

FRENCH TOASTED WAFFLES

Whisk together ¼ cup (60 ml/2 fl oz) milk and 2 eggs in a shallow dish. Dip 4–6 waffles, one at a time, into the mixture. Leave the waffles for just a few seconds each side, so that they soak up the egg mixture but don't become so soggy they break up. Melt a little butter in a non-stick frying pan. When the butter is foaming, add two or three of the waffles to the pan. Cook for 2–3 minutes each side, or until lightly golden brown and puffed and the egg mixture has cooked through. Serve immediately, dusted with icing sugar and topped with ice cream and maple syrup and sliced fresh strawberries. Serves 4–6.

CINNAMON WAFFLES

Grill 4 waffles under a preheated grill until golden brown. Brush one side liberally with melted butter and sprinkle with some caster sugar and ground cinnamon. Place under the grill again for about 30 seconds, then turn the waffles over and cook the other side. Serve immediately as they are, or with some fresh berries and a spoonful of mascarpone. Serves 2–4.

HOT BUTTERED CARAMEL WAFFLES

Toast 4 waffles on each side until golden brown. Heat 80 g (2⅔ oz) butter in a non-stick frying pan. When the butter is foaming, add the waffles, turning quickly to coat in butter. Remove from the pan and keep the waffles warm in a low oven, taking care not to let them become soggy. Working quickly, sprinkle 4 tablespoons soft brown sugar into the pan, stirring into the remaining butter. Add ⅔ cup (170 ml/5½ fl oz) cream and 2 tablespoons rum or brandy. Simmer for 1–2 minutes. Serve the sauce spooned over the buttered waffles with a scoop of ice cream. Serves 2–4.

WAFFLES WITH WHIPPED VANILLA RICOTTA

Beat 250 g (8 oz) fresh ricotta cheese with electric beaters until smooth. Add 2–3 teaspoons sugar and 2 teaspoons vanilla essence. If you wish, add a little finely grated orange, lemon or lime rind. Beat until combined. Alternatively, place the ingredients in a food processor and process to combine. Toast 4 waffles until golden brown on each side. Serve the toasted waffles with stewed or sautéed apples and the Whipped Vanilla Ricotta. Serves 2–4.

Clockwise from top left: Cinnamon Waffles;
Waffles with Vanilla Whipped Ricotta;
Hot Buttered Caramel Waffles;
French Toasted Waffles

SUN-DRIED TOMATO AND FETA WAFFLES WITH ROCKET SALAD

Preparation time: 35 minutes
Total cooking time: 25 minutes
Makes 6 waffles

1 cup (130 g/4^{1}/$_4$ oz) buckwheat flour
1 cup (125 g/4 oz) plain flour
2^{1}/$_2$ teaspoons baking powder
2 eggs
1^{3}/$_4$ cups (440 ml/14 fl oz) milk
100 g (3^{1}/$_3$ oz) butter, melted

100 g (3^{1}/$_3$ oz) sun-dried tomatoes, chopped
125 g (4 oz) feta cheese, crumbled

Rocket Salad
150 g (4^{3}/$_4$ oz) rocket
4 hard-boiled eggs, quartered
50 g (1^{2}/$_3$ oz) Parmesan cheese, shaved
2 tablespoons balsamic vinegar
2 tablespoons olive oil

1 Preheat the waffle iron. Sift the flours, baking powder and a pinch of salt into a bowl and make a well in the centre. Whisk the eggs, milk and butter in a jug and gradually pour into the well, whisking until just smooth. Fold in the tomatoes and feta.
2 Brush both surfaces of the waffle iron with melted butter. Pour ^{1}/$_2$ cup (125 ml/4 fl oz) batter into the centre and spread almost to the corners of the grid. Cook for 4 minutes, or until crisp and golden. Keep warm while cooking the remaining mixture.
3 To make Rocket Salad: Gently toss the rocket, eggs and Parmesan in a bowl. Whisk the balsamic vinegar and oil together, drizzle over the salad and serve with the waffles.

Pour the liquid into the well in the centre of the dry ingredients.

Gradually fold the sun-dried tomatoes and crumbled feta into the batter.

Cook the waffle for about 4 minutes, or until crisp and golden.

Peel and core the apples and then chop them roughly.

Simmer the apple mixture for 20 minutes or until the apple has softened.

CHEESE AND SMOKED HAM WAFFLES WITH CHILLI APPLE CHUTNEY

Preparation time: 45 minutes
Total cooking time: 30–40 minutes
Makes 6 waffles

Chilli Apple Chutney
1 tablespoon oil
1 onion, finely chopped
1 teaspoon cumin seeds
2 green apples (preferably granny smiths), peeled, cored and chopped
1 green chilli, finely chopped
1/2 cup (60 g/2 oz) sultanas
2 tablespoons soft brown sugar
2 tablespoons white vinegar

70 g (2 1/3 oz) butter
3 spring onions, finely chopped
2 cups (250 g/8 oz) plain flour
1/2 teaspoon baking powder
90 g (3 oz) red Leicester cheese, grated
100 g (3 1/3 oz) smoked ham, finely chopped
2 eggs, separated
1 1/3 cups (350 ml/11 fl oz) milk
2 teaspoons Dijon mustard

1 For Chilli Apple Chutney: Heat the oil in a pan and fry the onion and cumin seeds for 1–2 minutes, or until golden. Add the apple, chilli, sultanas, sugar and vinegar; bring to the boil, reduce the heat and simmer, covered, for 20 minutes, or until softened.

2 Heat a little of the butter in a small pan, add the spring onions and fry for 1 minute. Remove from the heat.

3 Preheat the waffle iron. Sift the flour and baking powder into a bowl, add the cheese and ham and make a well in the centre. Whisk together the egg yolks, milk, mustard, spring onions, remaining butter, melted, and salt and pepper in a jug and slowly pour into the well, whisking until the batter is just smooth.

4 Beat the egg whites into firm peaks. Stir a tablespoon of egg white into the batter to loosen it, then fold in the remainder. Brush both surfaces of the waffle iron with melted butter. Pour 1/2 cup (125 ml/4 fl oz) of batter into the centre of the waffle iron and spread almost to the corners of the grid. Close the lid and cook for about 1–2 minutes, or until golden. Keep the waffles warm while cooking the remaining batter. Serve warm with the Chilli Apple Chutney.

Add the egg mixture to the well in the centre of the dry ingredients.

Use a metal spoon to carefully fold the remaining egg whites into the batter.

COOK'S FILE

Note: The Chutney can be made up to a week in advance and stored in an airtight container in the refrigerator.

PARMESAN WAFFLES WITH RICOTTA AND BAKED TOMATOES

Preparation time: 25 minutes
Total cooking time: 2 hours
Makes 6 waffles

12 egg (Roma) tomatoes
1 tablespoon olive oil
1 tablespoon balsamic vinegar
500 g (1 lb) fresh ricotta
1/2 cup (125 g/4 oz) sour cream
2 tablespoons chopped chives
1 tablespoon each chopped mint, parsley, basil and thyme
2 cups (250 g/8 oz) self-raising flour
1/2 cup (50 g/1²/3 oz) freshly grated Parmesan cheese
2 spring onions, chopped
2 eggs, separated
3/4 cup (185 ml/6 fl oz) milk
1/2 cup (125 ml/4 fl oz) water
90 g (3 oz) butter, melted

1 Preheat the oven to slow 150°C (300°F/Gas 2). Cut the tomatoes in half lengthways and place in a baking dish. Bake for 45 minutes. Brush with the combined oil and vinegar and bake a further 45 minutes–1 hour, or until soft. Brush with oil and vinegar 2–3 times during cooking time.
2 With a wooden spoon, beat together the ricotta cheese, sour cream, herbs, salt and pepper, to taste, in a bowl.
3 Preheat the waffle iron. Combine the flour, Parmesan and spring onion in a bowl; make a well in the centre. Whisk the yolks, milk, water and butter in a jug and pour into the well, stirring until just smooth. Beat the egg whites with electric beaters until firm peaks form. Stir a tablespoon of egg white into the batter to loosen it, then fold in the remainder.
4 Brush both surfaces of the heated waffle iron with melted butter. Pour 1/2 cup (125 ml/4 fl oz) of the batter into the centre of the waffle iron and spread almost to the corners of the grid. Cook for 2–3 minutes, or until crisp and golden. Keep warm while cooking the remaining batter. Serve the waffles warm with the tomatoes and ricotta mixture.

Brush the partially cooked tomatoes with the combined oil and vinegar.

Beat the ricotta, sour cream, herbs, salt and pepper together in a bowl.

Pour the liquid into the well in the dry ingredients and stir with a metal spoon.

HASH BROWN WAFFLES

Preparation time: 25 minutes
Total cooking time: 40 minutes
Makes 4 waffles

4 potatoes
300 ml (9²/3 fl oz) milk
60 g (2 oz) butter, melted
2 eggs, lightly beaten

2 tablespoons chopped chives or parsley
1³/4 cups (185 g/6 oz) self-raising flour
¹/2 teaspoon salt

1 Boil the unpeeled potatoes until almost cooked but still firm. When cold, peel and coarsely grate.

2 Preheat a waffle iron. Combine the potato, milk, butter, eggs and chives or parsley. Stir in the flour and salt.

3 Brush both surfaces of the waffle iron with melted butter. Pour 1 cup (250 ml/8 fl oz) batter into the centre of the iron and spread almost to the corners of the grid. Cook for 5 minutes, or until brown and crisp. Keep warm while cooking the remaining batter. Delicious served with crispy bacon, grilled tomatoes and chutney.

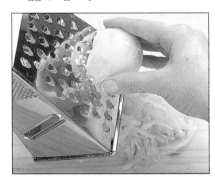

Cool the potatoes, then peel and grate coarsely with a metal grater.

Stir the flour and salt into the combined potato, milk, butter, eggs and chives.

Pour the batter into the centre of the waffle iron.

KUMERA WAFFLES WITH FRIED APPLE RINGS

Preparation time: 35 minutes
Total cooking time: 30–35 minutes
Makes 5 waffles

4 green apples, peeled
60 g (2 oz) unsalted butter
1/2 cup (115 g/3³/4 oz) firmly
　　packed soft brown sugar,
　　plus 1¹/2 tablespoons
1/4 teaspoon ground cinnamon
1/2 teaspoon salt
1¹/4 cups (315 ml/10 fl oz) milk
60 g (2 oz) butter, melted
2 eggs
2 cups (250 g/8 oz) self-raising
　　flour
3/4 cup (185 g/6 oz) cooked,
　　mashed kumera (orange
　　sweet potato)
10 slices crispy bacon or
　　prosciutto

1 Core and slice the apples into rings. Melt the unsalted butter in a heavy-based pan. Toss in the apples, cover and cook for 8 minutes over medium heat. Sprinkle with the sugar (reserving the 1¹/2 tablespoons) and cinnamon and cook for 8–10 minutes.
2 Preheat the waffle iron. Whisk the salt, milk, butter and eggs in a bowl. Whisk in the remaining sugar, flour and kumera until just smooth.
3 Brush both surfaces of the heated waffle iron with melted butter. Pour 1/2 cup (125 ml/4 fl oz) batter onto the iron and spread almost to the corners of the grid. Cook for 4–5 minutes, or until golden and crisp. Keep warm while cooking the remaining batter. Serve warm with the fried apple and crispy bacon or prosciutto.

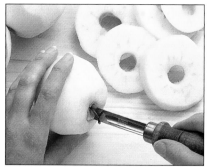

Use an apple corer to remove the cores from each of the apples.

Sprinkle the partially cooked apples with the brown sugar and cinnamon.

Whisk the remaining brown sugar, flour and kumera into the egg mixture.

MEXICAN WAFFLES

Preparation time: 35 minutes
Total cooking time: 45 minutes
Makes 5–6 waffles

2 x 425 g (13¹/₂ oz) cans red
    kidney beans, drained
1 cup (250 ml/8 fl oz) vegetable
    stock
2 onions, diced
2 cloves garlic, chopped
3 carrots, peeled and diced
2 teaspoons cumin seeds
¹/₄ cup (60 ml/2 fl oz) tomato
    sauce
3 tablespoons tomato paste
2 tablespoons red wine vinegar

2 cups (250 g/8 oz) plain flour
1 tablespoon baking powder
2 eggs
300 ml (9²/₃ fl oz) milk
¹/₃ cup (80 ml/2³/₄ fl oz) oil
2 sliced avocados, grated
    Cheddar cheese, sour cream
    and paprika, to serve

1 Place the beans and stock in a large pan and add the onion, garlic, carrot and cumin seeds. Cook for 30 minutes, or until tender. Stir in the tomato sauce, paste and vinegar and cook for 15 minutes. Season with salt and pepper, and keep warm.
2 Preheat the waffle iron. Sift the flour, baking powder and a pinch of salt into a bowl and make a well in the

centre. Whisk the eggs, milk and oil in a jug and stir into the well until just smooth. Brush both surfaces of the waffle iron with melted butter. Pour ¹/₂ cup (125 ml/4 fl oz) batter into the centre of the iron and spread almost to the corners of the grid. Cook for 5 minutes, or until crisp. Keep warm while cooking the remaining mixture.
3 Spoon the bean mixture over the waffles, arrange avocado on top and sprinkle with cheese. Place under a grill until the cheese melts. Top with sour cream and dust with paprika.

COOK'S FILE

Note: A shake of Tabasco sauce will spice up the beans. Serve with chopped lettuce, if desired.

Stir the tomato sauce, tomato paste and the vinegar into the bean mixture.

Add the egg mixture to the well in the dry ingredients and stir until just smooth.

Pour the batter into the heated waffle iron and spread to the corners.

CORN WAFFLES WITH TOMATO SALSA

Preparation time: 30 minutes
Total cooking time: 20 minutes
Makes 6 waffles

Tomato Salsa
4 tomatoes, diced
1/2 cup (15 g/1/2 oz) coriander
   leaves
1 small red onion, chopped
2 spring onions, chopped
1 tablespoon red wine vinegar
1/2–1 jalapeno chilli, seeded and
   chopped
1/2 teaspoon sugar

2 cups (250 g/8 oz) plain flour
1 tablespoon baking powder
1 teaspoon salt
2 eggs
1 1/4 cups (315 ml/10 fl oz) milk
1/4 cup (60 ml/2 fl oz) oil
410 g (13 oz) can corn kernels,
   drained
2 tablespoons chopped parsley
   or chives
1/4 cup (25 g/3/4 oz) Parmesan,
   grated

1 To make Tomato Salsa: Put the tomato, coriander leaves, onion, spring onion, vinegar, chilli and sugar in a food processor and pulse until coarsely chopped. Pour into a bowl, season to taste with salt and pepper, and cover.

2 Preheat a waffle iron. Sift the flour, baking powder and salt into a bowl. Whisk the eggs, milk and oil in a jug and stir into the dry ingredients until just smooth. Fold in the corn, parsley or chives and Parmesan.

3 Brush both surfaces of the heated waffle iron with melted butter. Pour 1/2 cup of the corn batter into the centre of the waffle iron and spread almost to the corners of the grid. Cook for 3–4 minutes, or until the waffle is golden and crisp. Keep warm while cooking the remaining batter. Serve the waffles warm with a little of the Tomato Salsa.

Wear rubber gloves (to prevent burning) to seed and chop the chilli.

Combine all the salsa ingredients in a food processor.

Fold the corn kernels, chopped herbs and Parmesan cheese into the batter.

HAM AND CHEESE WAFFLES

Preparation time: 20 minutes
Total cooking time: 25–30 minutes
Makes 4–5 waffles

2 cups (250 g/8 oz) plain flour
1 tablespoon baking powder
1 teaspoon salt
2 eggs, beaten

1/3 cup (80 ml/2 3/4 fl oz) oil
1 1/4 cups (315 ml/10 fl oz) milk
2 teaspoons wholegrain mustard
1/2 cup (60 g/2 oz) grated
   Cheddar cheese
2 tablespoons chopped parsley
1/2 cup (80 g/2 2/3 oz) coarsely
   chopped ham

1 Preheat a waffle iron. Sift the flour, baking powder and salt into a large bowl and make a well in the centre.

2 Whisk the eggs, oil, milk, mustard, cheese and parsley in a jug. Pour into the well and whisk until just smooth.

3 Brush both surfaces of the waffle iron with melted butter. Pour 1/2 cup (125 ml/4 fl oz) batter into the iron and spread almost to the corners of the grid. Sprinkle with 1 tablespoon ham and cook for 4–5 minutes, or until golden and crisp. Keep warm while cooking the remaining mixture. Delicious with sliced tomatoes.

Whisk the eggs, oil, milk, mustard, cheese and parsley with a fork.

Add the egg mixture to the well in the centre of the dry ingredients.

Top each uncooked waffle with a little chopped ham before closing the lid.

Corn Waffles with Tomato Salsa (top)
with Ham and Cheese Waffles

CHILLI AND CORIANDER WAFFLES WITH TOFU

Preparation time: 25 minutes
Total cooking time: 30 minutes
Makes 4

Marinated Tofu
350 g (11¼ oz) firm tofu, cut
    into 1 cm (½ inch)-thick
    triangles
1 tablespoon grated fresh ginger
2 spring onions, finely chopped
1 tablespoon mirin
¼ cup (60 ml/2 fl oz) soy sauce
1 teaspoon sesame oil

2 cups (250 g/8 oz) plain flour
2 teaspoons baking powder
125 g (4 oz) peanuts, roasted
    and finely ground
400 ml (12⅔ fl oz) coconut milk
2 eggs
1 tablespoon grated lime rind
30 g (1 oz) butter, melted
2 teaspoons sambal oelek
½ cup (15 g/½ oz) coriander
    leaves

1 **To make Marinated Tofu:**
Place the tofu in a bowl and pour over
the combined ginger, spring onion,
mirin, soy sauce and sesame oil. Cover
and refrigerate for 2 hours. Drain well
and reserve the marinade. Just before
serving, cook the tofu in a non-stick
pan over high heat for 3 minutes, or
until golden brown.
2 Preheat the waffle iron. Sift the
flour and baking powder into a bowl,
add the peanuts and make a well in
the centre. Whisk the coconut milk,
eggs, lime rind, melted butter and
sambal oelek in a jug and gradually
pour into the well, whisking until just
smooth. Fold in the coriander.
3 Brush both surfaces of the heated
waffle iron with melted butter. Pour
½ cup (125 ml/4 fl oz) batter into the
centre of the iron and spread with the
back of a spoon almost to the corners
of the grid. Close the iron and cook the
waffle for 3–5 minutes, or until crisp
and golden. Remove and keep warm
while cooking the remaining batter.
4 Divide the waffles among 4 plates.
Top with the fried tofu, drizzle with
the reserved marinade and garnish
with a few sliced spring onions.

Pour the combined ginger, spring onions, mirin, soy sauce and oil over the tofu.

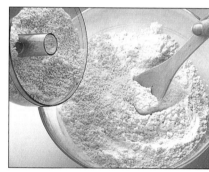

Add the ground peanuts to the sifted flour and baking powder.

Using a metal spoon, fold the coriander leaves into the batter.

Pour ½ cup (125 ml/4 fl oz) of batter into the waffle iron, then spread evenly.

CREAMY SCRAMBLED EGGS WITH SMOKED SALMON ON WAFFLES

Preparation time: 25 minutes
Total cooking time: 25 minutes
Makes 5–6 waffles

2 cups (250 g/8 oz) plain flour
1 tablespoon baking powder
1 teaspoon salt
2 eggs
300 ml (9²/3 fl oz) milk
1/3 cup (80 ml/2³/4 fl oz) oil

Scrambled Eggs
6 eggs
1 cup (250 ml/8 fl oz) milk or
 cream, or half and half
45 g (1¹/2 oz) butter, melted
200 g (6¹/2 oz) smoked salmon,
 thinly sliced
1 tablespoon chopped chives
cracked black pepper

1 Preheat a waffle iron. Sift the flour, baking powder and salt into a bowl; make a well in the centre. Whisk the eggs, milk and oil in a jug and pour into the well, whisking until smooth.

2 Brush both surfaces of the waffle iron with melted butter. Pour 1/2 cup (125 ml/4 fl oz) batter into the centre of the iron and spread almost to the corners of the grid. Cook for 5 minutes or until brown and crisp. Keep warm while cooking the remaining batter.

3 To make Scrambled Eggs: Whisk the eggs, milk, cream and butter together. Pour into a pan and cook over medium heat; stir occasionally. Just before the egg sets, stir in the salmon, chives and pepper. Remove from the heat to prevent overcooking. Serve with hot waffles.

Add the egg mixture to the well in the centre of the dry ingredients.

Cook the waffles for 5 minutes, or until brown and crisp.

Stir in the salmon and chives just before the mixture sets.

POLENTA WAFFLES WITH RED PEPPER AND BASIL BUTTER

Preparation time: 35 minutes
Total cooking time: 20 minutes
Makes 7 waffles

Red Pepper and Basil Butter
125 g (4 oz) butter, softened
1/4 cup (40 g/1 1/3 oz) finely chopped red capsicum
1 tablespoon finely chopped fresh basil
1 clove garlic, crushed

2 cups (250 g/8 oz) plain flour
1/2 teaspoon baking powder
1 cup (150 g/4 3/4 oz) fine polenta
2 tablespoons caster sugar
3 eggs, separated
1 1/2 cups (375 ml/12 fl oz) buttermilk
60 g (2 oz) butter, melted

1 To make Red Pepper and Basil Butter: Mix the butter, capsicum, basil and garlic in a food processor until smooth. Scrape the butter onto a sheet of foil and wrap into a cylinder shape, twisting the ends tightly. Refrigerate until firm. To serve, unwrap and cut into thin slices.

2 Preheat the waffle iron. Sift the flour and baking powder into a bowl. Add the polenta and sugar and make a well in the centre. Whisk the egg yolks, buttermilk and melted butter in a jug and gradually pour into the well, whisking until just smooth.

3 Beat the egg whites in a small clean dry bowl with electric beaters until firm peaks form (any grease in the bowl will prevent the eggs aerating). Stir a tablespoon of the egg white into the batter to loosen it up, then gently fold in the remainder.

4 Brush both surfaces of a heated waffle iron with melted butter. Pour 1/2 cup (125 ml/4 fl oz) batter into the centre of the iron and spread almost to the corners of the grid. Close the lid and cook for 1–2 minutes, or until golden. Remove the waffle and keep warm while cooking the remaining batter. Serve the waffles with slices of chilled Red Pepper and Basil Butter.

Unwrap the butter when it is firm and cut into thin slices.

Add the polenta and sugar to the sifted flour and baking powder.

Add the egg mixture to the well in the centre of the dry ingredients.

Use a spoon to spread the batter almost to the corners of the grid.

INDEX

INTERNATIONAL GLOSSARY OF INGREDIENTS

caster sugar	superfine sugar	self-raising flour	self-rising flour
apricot nectar	apricot juice	choc bits	chocolate chips
demerara sugar	raw sugar	icing sugar	confectioners' sugar
unsalted butter	sweet butter	ground almonds	almond meal
eggplant	aubergine	plain flour	all-purpose flour
cream	single/light cream	bicarbonate of soda	baking soda
thick cream	double/heavy cream	capsicum	green or red pepper
cornflour	cornstarch	plain chocolate	dark chocolate
zucchini	courgette	kumera	orange sweet potato

Published by Murdoch Books®, a division of Murdoch Magazines Pty Limited,
213 Miller Street, North Sydney NSW 2060.

Managing Editor: Jane Price. **Food Editors:** Roslyn Anderson, Kerrie Ray, Dimitra Stais, Jody Vassallo. **Editors:** Penny McGregor, Alison Moss. **Designer:** Michèle Lichtenberger. **Recipe Development:** Amanda Cooper, Michelle Earl, Rosemary Mellish, Jody Vassallo. **Food Stylist:** Carolyn Fienberg. **Photographers:** Jon Bader, Reg Morrison (steps). **Food Preparation:** Jo Forrest. **Home Economists:** Michelle Lawton, Kerrie Mullins.
Publisher: Anne Wilson. **International Sales Director:** Mark Newman.
National Library of Australia Cataloguing-in-Publication Data. Pancakes, pikelets, crepes and waffles. Includes index. ISBN 0 86411 549 0. 1. Pancakes, waffles, etc. (Series: Family circle step-by-step.) 641.815. First printed 1997. Printed by Prestige Litho, Queensland.